PMW BH5-10

WITHDRAWN

148093

A NATIONAL LABOR POLICY

THE BROOKINGS INSTITUTION

The Brookings Institution—Devoted to Public Service through Research and Training in the Social Sciences—was incorporated on December 8, 1927. Broadly stated, the Institution has two primary purposes: the first is to aid constructively in the development of sound national policies; and the second is to offer training of a super-graduate character to students of the social sciences.

The responsibility of the final determination of the Institution's policies and its program of work for the administration of its endowment is vested in a self-perpetuating board of trustees. It is the function of the trustees to make possible the conduct of scientific research under the most favorable conditions, and to safeguard the independence of the research staff in the pursuit of their studies and in the publication of the results of such studies. It is not a part of their function to determine, control, or influence the conduct of particular investigations or the conclusions reached, but only to approve the principal fields of investigation to which the available funds are to be allocated, and to satisfy themselves with reference to the intellectual competence and scientific integrity of the staff. Major responsibility for "formulating general policies and co-ordinating the activities of the Institution" is vested in the president. The by-laws provide also that "there shall be an advisory council selected by the president from among the scientific staff of the Institution."

Authors of studies published by the Institution have had the advice, criticism, and assistance both of an administrative officer and of a co-operating committee selected from the staff. In a manuscript accepted for publication, the author has freedom to present his final interpretations and conclusions, although they may not necessarily be concurred in by some or all of those who co-operate with him or by other members of the staff. The Institution in publishing the work assumes the responsibility that it meets reasonable tests of scholarship and presents data and conclusions worthy of public consideration.

A NATIONAL LABOR POLICY

BY

HAROLD W. METZ

AND

MEYER JACOBSTEIN

THE BROOKINGS INSTITUTION
WASHINGTON, D. C.

1947

Printed in the United States of America
Cornelius Printing Company
Silver Spring, Md.

PREFACE

During the last fifteen years public opinion with respect to labor has fluctuated widely. Before the great depression neither the public nor the government manifested much concern over the weak bargaining position of labor. But in the thirties the federal government, supported by public opinion, undertook to promote the extension of unionism throughout the economy, to broaden the scope of collective agreements, and in every possible way to increase the power of labor organizations in the bargaining process.

The ensuing increase in the scope of unionism not only changed the balance of power between labor and capital, but it also placed labor organizations and labor leaders in a dominant position in the whole economic and political system. Since the disappearance of wartime constraints, the capacity of organized labor to injure the general public, including unorganized workers, has become increasingly evident. The unprecedented wave of strikes in 1946 and the resulting disruptions of production convinced a large segment of the population that the power of labor organizations must be restrained to safeguard the public interest.

Foreseeing these trends, the Brookings Institution some three years ago began a systematic study of federal labor policy as manifested in the multitude of laws, administrative determinations, and court decisions relating to labor problems. In September 1945 the Institution published *The Labor Policy of the Federal Government,* by Harold W. Metz. This preliminary study was confined to the presentation of the facts.

The present study, undertaken jointly by Mr. Metz and Mr. Jacobstein of the Institution staff, appraises existing labor policies and makes concrete suggestions for appropriate modifications. The general position of the authors is that the collective bargaining process can be made an effective means of adjusting industrial differences and that the public interest

v

can at the same time be reasonably safeguarded. They set forth the reasons why, in their judgment, the alternative of compulsory adjustments of labor controversies is impracticable and why it would inevitably lead to increasing governmental interference with and control over both employers and employees.

The book is divided into three sections. Part I is a succinct historical summary of the evolution of federal labor policy over the last thirty years. In the two chapters which comprise Part II, the authors present the basic criteria by which they evaluate the various phases of labor policy. Part III is devoted to a detailed analysis of the major issues involved in the labor problem today. Each chapter arrives at specific conclusions and recommendations. The concluding chapter sets forth the alternatives between which the American government must now choose.

While the two authors have collaborated on the analysis as a whole, Mr. Jacobstein is primarily responsible for Chapters I, III, and VIII, and Mr. Metz for the remaining chapters.

Harold G. Moulton,
President

January 1947

CONTENTS

PAGE

PREFACE V

PART I. INTRODUCTION

I. THE BACKGROUND OF FEDERAL INTERVENTION.. 2
   The Traditional Policy of Independence.......... 2
   Influence of World War I.............................. 3
   Why Organized Labor Lost Ground in the
      1920's.. 4
   Protection of the Right to Organize on Rail-
      roads... 7
   Protection of Labor by the Anti-Injunction Act 9
   Government Guarantee of the Rights of Labor
      under NRA.. 11
   Labor's Basic Charter.................................... 14
   Influence of World War II.............................. 17

II. SUMMARY OF THE LABOR POLICY OF THE FED-
      ERAL GOVERNMENT....................................... 20
   Constitutional Difficulties 20
   Principles Underlying Government Policy........ 22
      Promoting concerted action...................... 22
      Protecting the right of self-organization.... 25
      The settlement of disputes....................... 26
      The dominant emphasis upon bargaining
         power 26

III. POLITICAL ASPECTS OF THE LABOR MOVEMENT.. 31
   The Voting Power of Labor............................ 31
   Industry-Wide Strikes and Government Inter-
      vention 32
   Collective Bargaining at the White House...... 34
   Labor Politics in Administration of Labor Laws 42
   Labor Resists Changes in the Wagner Act...... 44
   The Influence of Labor in Nonenforcement of
      Laws 45

PART II. NATIONAL GOALS AND REQUIREMENTS

CHAPTER   PAGE

IV. Basic National Goals and Conceptions........   50
    An ever-expanding national income..........   50
    Progressively wider distribution of income   51
    Reduced effort in production......................   51
    Reward based on effort...............................   52
    Full development of individual capacities..   52
    Right of association..................................   53
    Avoidance of violence...............................   53
    Free speech...   53

V. Underlying Considerations in National La-
    bor Policy   55
    Labor Unions Perform a Necessary Function..   55
    Restrictive Labor Practices Are Undesirable....   58
    Collective Bargaining Should Be Between an
      Employer and His Employees......................   61
    Labor Conflicts Should Not Be Extended to
      Injure Innocent Third Parties.....................   64
    Machinery Should Exist to Encourage the
      Peaceful Settlement of Disputes...................   65

PART III. A NATIONAL LABOR POLICY

VI. The Right to Organize..............................   69
    Protecting the Right to Organize.....................   69
    Railway Labor Act.....................................   69
    National Labor Relations Act.....................   70
    Recommendations   76
    Union Preference   79
    Summary...   84

VII. Strikes, Picketing, and Boycotts..............   85
    Strikes   85
    Recommendations   91
    Picketing   92
    Boycotts...   94
    Recommendations   96

CHAPTER   PAGE

VIII. COLLECTIVE BARGAINING 98
    Collective Bargaining under the Wagner Act.... 98
    How the National Labor Relations Board Interprets the Law... 99
    Labor not Obligated to Bargain Collectively.... 103
    The Scope of Bargaining Agreements.............. 105
    Collective Bargaining Under the Railway Labor Act 106
    Difficulties in the Enforcement of Labor Agreements.. 107
    Recommendations 109

IX. THE GOVERNMENT AND THE BARGAINING UNIT.. 110
    Significance of the Bargaining Unit.................. 111
    The National Labor Relations Board and the Bargaining Unit 113
    Multiple-Employer Bargaining Units................ 117
    Recommendations 120

X. THE ORGANIZATION OF UNIONS....................... 124

XI. THE ORGANIZATION OF THE NATIONAL LABOR RELATIONS BOARD... 129
    Defects in the Present Machinery.................... 129
    Recommendation 134

XII. THE SETTLEMENT OF DISPUTES...................... 136
    The National Labor Relations Act.................... 136
    The Conciliation Service.................................. 137
    Railway Labor Disputes.................................... 139
    The National War Labor Board....................... 143
    The President and Labor Disputes.................... 146
    Compulsory Cooling-Off Period....................... 146
    Summary... 147

XIII. HOW CAN INDUSTRIAL DISPUTES BE SETTLED?.. 150
    Compulsory Settlements 151
    Collective Bargaining 155
    Protection of the Public 158

The study upon which this book is based was made possible by funds granted by The Maurice and Laura Falk Foundation of Pittsburgh. However, the Falk Foundation is not the author, publisher, or proprietor of this publication and is not to be understood as approving or disapproving by virtue of its grant any of the statements and views expressed herein.

PART I

INTRODUCTION

Part I, consisting of three chapters, provides background as well as material essential to an understanding of existing federal labor policies.

Chapter I traces the origin and the development of our federal labor laws. We note that changing economic forces brought about a radical departure in the attitude of trade unions toward government interference in labor relations. Attention is called to the rise of the industrial type of union organization, which resulted in a split in the organized labor movement. Finally, we indicate the factors that led to the emergence of a new attitude on the part of government with respect to labor policy.

Chapter II contains a summary statement, in broad terms, of existing federal labor policies. Since it is based upon the detailed study recently published by the Institution under the title the *Labor Policy of the Federal Government,* no specific documentation is given. The purpose of the chapter is purely expository. In Part III a detailed analysis and appraisal of the various aspects of our federal labor policies will be presented.

In Chapter III we call attention to the political implications of our federal labor program. We show how and why the labor movement has become increasingly political in character. The chapter traces the intervention of the federal government in the settlement of labor disputes, which followed as a consequence of the close connection between organized labor and national politics, and reveals that the political influence of the labor bloc has grown strong enough to resist modifications in our labor legislation.

CHAPTER I

THE BACKGROUND OF FEDERAL INTERVENTION

During the last half-century we have witnessed the introduction in the United States of mass production industries and ever-widening markets. These important economic developments have had an impact on the organized labor movement, forcing it to undergo changes in the structure and policy of labor unions. This, in turn, has led to the adoption of a new government labor relations policy. The major events in its evolution will be traced in this chapter.

THE TRADITIONAL POLICY OF INDEPENDENCE

The role of the federal government in the labor field is of recent origin. Labor had long viewed congressional action with suspicion, since it feared that employer and financial interests dictated to the major political parties. It was the traditional policy of national unions organized along craft lines to place their main reliance on self-help and voluntary action. The American Federation of Labor, of which 100 or more national unions are constituent parts, has adhered consistently, from its inception in 1886 down to 1926, to the general policy of noninterference by the federal government in the determination of wages and working conditions. Samuel Gompers, the first president of the Federation and, except for one term, leader until the time of his death in 1924, resisted alliances with any political party and refrained from calling on Congress for aid in fighting the battles of labor. Organized labor did endorse candidates who were considered friendly to labor. The Gompers philosophy was adopted as a sound one by his successor, William Green.

The AFL, however, exerted no little influence in shaping state legislation. It sponsored and fought for legislation concerning workmen's accident compensation, safety laws, restriction of hours of labor for women and children, prison labor, and the general welfare. Except for groups not able to protect themselves through their own organized efforts, the Federation refrained from calling upon the state governments for direct aid in unionization and collective bargaining.

Until quite recently, the 1930's, American unions were primarily, if not exclusively, craft unions. Skilled workers in each industry united for self-protection and for improving their working conditions and standards of living. They sought to exercise a semimonopoly power in their respective fields. Entrance into the crafts was controlled by strict apprenticeship rules. These separate craft unions, local or national, guarded with a jealous eye the area of operations over which each claimed special jurisdiction. They fought for union recognition and collective bargaining, using as weapons the strike, picketing, and the boycott. Their major objective was to strengthen their bargaining position. The goal of labor was not broad social and economic changes.

For nearly fifty years the AFL pursued this general policy. Its success was limited to those industries in which skills predominated. The Federation made little headway among the semiskilled and much less among the unskilled. Prior to World War I its total membership was approximately 2.5 millions, which was a small fraction of the total work force and only a relatively small percentage of all industrial workers. The highest degree of unionization was achieved among the skilled workers on railroads, in the various building trades, the printing and garment industries, and in the northern coal mining industry.

INFLUENCE OF WORLD WAR I

Labor's first experience with federal intervention came during the first World War. At the request of President Wilson, representatives of the AFL met with employers in a labor conference, at which was formulated a set of principles to be used as a guide during the war emergency. The basic ideas agreed to by both parties were that labor would not strike, and in return that employers would recognize the right of labor to organize; and, moreover, employers would refrain from discriminating against union workers or those desiring to unionize. The program was administered by a National War Labor Board composed of twelve members, five representing labor, five the employers, and two the public. The National War Labor Board protected labor against employer discrimination; but the Board refused to impose the closed shop.

WHY ORGANIZED LABOR LOST GROUND IN THE 1920's

After the United States entered the first World War trade union membership increased from about 3 millions to about 5 millions. This growth was mainly in industries in which unions had been relatively strong before the war: transportation, construction, metal trades, clothing, and ship-building. In spite of increased power resulting from the war experience, the AFL reverted after the war to its traditional policy of self-help, self-determination, and direct action in unionization and collective bargaining. The tight labor market following the close of hostilities encouraged the AFL in the belief that labor could prosper without the aid of the federal government. It did not request the continuation of the wartime labor policy of the government. Wages rose in the period immediately following the war. Unionization made some headway in a few lines, for example, in the garment trades. It was traditional union doctrine that unions gained strength during prosperous times.

Labor leaders who looked forward to a long period of full business activity were soon disillusioned. The tight labor market and the business activity continued less than two years. Then came the depression of 1920–21. Unemployment set in and wages were cut in nearly all industries. In some cases this led to strikes on a large scale as in the railway, steel, and soft coal industries. Many of the strikes during this period were unsuccessful. Workers began dropping out of unions which they had joined during the war. Women had entered industry and had become unionized, but with the onset of the depression, they left their jobs. By 1923 the total union membership had dropped from the 5 million mark of 1920 to 3.6 millions. In these three years the loss in membership wiped out half of the wartime gains.

When business activity resumed and the boom period set in, union leaders were confronted with an unprecedented situation. Industry entered a period of rapid and extensive introduction of labor-saving machinery. Technological changes extended the development of mass production. Scientific management in the hands of industrial engineers caused worry among labor leaders. Unskilled labor was drawn into industries in large numbers. Women displaced men in many of the highly mechanized factories. Job analysis by engineers led to a high degree of specialization. This industrial process involved nothing startling, except that the changes came very rapidly and covered a large area of our economy. There was considerable temporary unemployment in certain industries where technological changes were made. In many instances production was increased with a reduced work force. The net effect of the technical changes was to minimize the importance of skills. Obviously this reacted unfavorably upon craft unions.

The process of unionization was made even more difficult by the considerable shift of industry geographically. For example, many of the New England textile mills moved to the South, where organized labor had not yet gained a strong foothold. Another obstacle to union organization was the fact that the standard of living of workers had improved during this period. Real wages increased since wages rose faster than the cost of living. In spite of the considerable amount of technological displacement, the over-all employment situation was favorable with less than 3 millions unemployed in 1929. The period was one of intense activity with expansion in old industries and development in new ones. There was also a strong movement toward concentration not only in production but in ownership.

The industrial and management changes put organized labor on the defensive. Moreover, the employers in many areas and in a number of industries opened a counter-attack on unionism. The program was well planned and highly organized and received the support of many employer associations. This antiunion movement, labeled the "American Plan", had as its objective the open shop. It was frankly avowed an aggressive attack on unionism. In some communities employers set up employment clearing offices, where individual employee records were kept, so that applicants for jobs who might be suspected of having union leanings could be black-listed. In many plants undercover men were engaged by employers to ferret out employees who belonged to unions or who displayed any interest in union organization activities. These antiunion techniques were of course legal; while under the law workers had a right to organize unions, it was equally legal for the employer to refuse to employ union men or applicants suspected of having union sympathies.

Management, however, was not content with pursuing antiunion techniques in its effort to avoid dealing with outside unions. Many employers inaugurated plans for more intelligent handling of labor matters. Industry began to realize that a considerable amount of discontent among its workers arose frequently from the unintelligent and arbitrary action of foremen. To rectify this situation, employment managers were engaged to devote their time exclusively to the problems of labor. These managers were vested with authority to hire, discharge, and discipline workers, and also to help in the establishment of fair wages and working conditions. Scientific methods of determining piece rates were introduced, and the employment manager was responsible for seeing that the time studies were fair. Welfare and organizational activities were introduced in many large plants to develop plant loyalty among the work force.

As a further means of preventing outside unions from getting a foothold, management encouraged and financed inside company unions. The officers of these unions had to be employees of the firm, and management conferred with them on matters affecting wages and working conditions. The union acted in a purely advisory capacity, and the employer made the final decision. Company unions, or as they are sometimes called employee representation plans, covered a wide range of industries including public utilities, steel mills, transportation, chemicals, machinery, and many others. The rapid growth of the company union in a few years from a membership of 1 million or 1.5 millions is significant when it is compared with the growth of regular trade unions to a membership of a little less than 3.5 millions in nearly a century. The trade unions were not blind to the importance of this trend. The status of the company-dominated union, therefore, became one of the troublesome points in the federal labor laws enacted during the Roosevelt administration.

The industrial changes in the 1920's had an impact on the character of labor organization. With the growth of mass production industries, labor began to organize along industrial rather than craft lines. The AFL, however, stuck stubbornly to its traditional basis of craft organization. Its refusal to adjust to the new industrial changes laid the ground work for the development of a new form of unionism and culminated in the founding of the Congress of Industrial Organizations in 1935. The struggle between the two types of organization led to many jurisdictional disputes that have plagued our industrial labor situation.

PROTECTION OF THE RIGHT TO ORGANIZE ON RAILROADS

The first important move in the direction of federal protection of the right to organize came with the enactment of the Railway Labor Act in 1926. From the point of view of labor this act was strengthened by amendments adopted in 1934. To understand how and why it came into being, one must know something of the background of the legislation. The government returned the railroads to private ownership in 1920. Simultaneously Congress created a tripartite Railroad Labor Board for the purpose of settling disputes. The Board was purely advisory, with powers to investigate and with authority to subpoena documents and compel the attendance of witnesses. It had no power to enforce decisions but relied solely on the force of public opinion to secure acceptance of its decisions.

The fact is, however, that both the railroads and the unions disregarded the recommendations in important cases. During the depression of 1920–21 wages were cut, and bitter and disastrous strikes ensued—including probably the most disastrous railroad strike the country has ever experienced. It was for the purpose of preventing strikes and avoiding interruption of railway service that the railroads and the unions jointly appealed to Congress to enact the Railway Labor Act of 1926. The major operating unions, the four brotherhoods, that embraced the engineers, conductors, firemen, and brakemen, which were unaffiliated with the AFL, joined with the various shop craft unions in urging the enactment of this law. The AFL departed from its traditional policies and also supported the proposal. The fact that many of the shopmen were members of the AFL probably accounts for this departure in policy. The lack of enthusiasm of the AFL for the principles of the Railway Labor Act is indicated by its failure to influence Congress in adapting these principles to industry. The record does not disclose any simultaneous effort on the part of Congress to apply the principles of the act to industry.

The Railway Labor Act created a Mediation Board, consisting of three full-time members appointed by the President. The Board and its staff seek to adjust disputes between the parties by voluntary agreement wherever possible. In the event this fails, the Board endeavors to have the parties submit the dispute to voluntary arbitration. Should this fail, and should it appear that the dispute might eventuate in a strike, the Board takes steps to have the President appoint a fact-finding commission. This step is recommended only in case of emergency.

The law imposes on both the railroads and the railroad unions the obligation to make every sincere effort to enter into and to maintain collective bargaining agreements, relating to wages, hours, working rules, and other employment conditions. The workers are protected by the law in the selection of their representatives. Under the law as amended in 1934, it is the function of the Board to supervise the selection of the bargaining unit. The employer is prohibited by law from interfering with the process of unionization and is not permitted to discriminate against union members. However the closed shop is prohibited, and individual workers are permitted to present their grievances without the intercession of the representative of a union.

PROTECTION OF LABOR BY THE ANTI-INJUNCTION ACT

The second major step in the development of the policy of federal intervention came with the enactment of the Norris-LaGuardia Anti-Injunction Act in 1932. This law imposed restrictions on the federal courts in the issuance of injunctions in labor disputes. Labor generally had been very critical and resentful of the use of injunctions against union activities. Temporary injunctions often granted without hearing labor's side of the case frequently had the effect of paralyzing the efforts of the organizers attempting to unionize a plant or conduct a successful strike. Restraining orders were especially effective in restricting the use of picketing. The Norris-LaGuardia Act, sponsored by organized labor, sought to rectify the alleged abuses by requiring the hearing of both parties before the issuance of an injunction by a federal court. The act also set forth specifically many activities against which a temporary or permanent restraining order could not be issued.

This statute made unenforceable in the federal courts what was commonly referred to by labor as the "yellow-dog contract." Under this contract an applicant for a job was required to withdraw his membership in an outside union and to agree not to join such union during the term of the employment contract. The use of such contracts was strenuously resisted by labor as being an infringement of a constitutional right, but the courts generally sustained the contracts until they were outlawed by the Norris-LaGuardia Act.

Aside from the specific provisions relating to injunctions and the yellow-dog contract, the Anti-Injunction Act had further significance. It contained the first declaration of a congressional labor policy with respect to collective bargaining for all cases coming within the jurisdiction of the federal courts.

Section 2 of the act declares that as a matter of basic policy employees should have full freedom of association; the right of self-organization; and the right to choose their own representatives without interference by employers; and finally, that the principle of collective bargaining is recognized. The fundamental concept of this act is that labor is the underdog and is unable through self-help alone, to achieve concerted action successfully and to wrest from the employers proper wages or fair labor conditions. Under this declared policy, the federal courts since 1940 have explicitly exempted labor unions from the operation of antitrust laws.

The law provided no devices or machinery, outside the federal courts, for the achievement of this general policy. It did, however, enunciate in section 2 a principle which influenced subsequent legislation. Organized labor was apparently content to secure legislative protection against the use of injunctions in labor disputes and the outlawing of the yellow-dog contract.

GOVERNMENT GUARANTEE OF THE RIGHTS OF LABOR
UNDER NRA

The long and disastrous depression which began in 1929 set the stage for a new series of laws applicable to industrial labor relations. The struggle of business enterprises to sell their merchandise in a highly competitive and declining market led to a rapid reduction in prices, followed by a cutting of wages and wage rates. Unemployment reached staggering figures. In the face of overwhelming deflationary forces, organized labor was powerless. In some fields, as in the construction industry, wage rates could be maintained. But maintaining union rates meant nothing to the workers if jobs were not available at such rates.

In this situation organized labor appealed to Congress to enact a law restricting work to thirty hours a week. The purpose was to spread the available work without a reduction in wages. This was the first time in the long history of the AFL that it had called on the federal government for aid in fixing the hours and wages of labor. Congress failed to enact the thirty-hour law but the labor leaders were committed to a new doctrine of federal intervention. In the critical emergency the policy of self-help had proved futile.

While the fight for the thirty-hour week was in progress, the Roosevelt administration was developing an entirely new program. It was a plan for general recovery not merely a labor program. The National Industrial Recovery Act, passed in June 1933, embodied the basic provisions of the plan. Labor groups played no role in initiating the recovery bill. The NIRA was only one step in the larger program for the use of federal functions in meeting many emergency problems. The New Deal extended these functions into many fields, affecting banking, the gold standard, stock-market operations, transportation, agriculture, and financial aid to distressed businesses. New activities were introduced, including public works, direct federal relief, and social security.

While the NIRA was primarily intended to reverse the downward spiral of deflation, it contained a labor provision which became the basis of the Wagner Labor Act. The NRA was made acceptable to labor by incorporating this labor section in the act. The recovery proposal was made acceptable to industry by permitting firms to organize trade associations with powers which, under normal circumstances, would come under the eye of the Justice Department as violations of the Anti-trust Act.

Each industry was permitted to establish a "code of fair competition" which, when approved by the President, had the full force of law. The code, however, had to contain provisions for labor standards for the entire industry, including minimum wages, maximum hours of labor, and such other terms as could be agreed upon in collective bargaining. This laid the groundwork for the Wagner Act.

It was section 7 (a) of the National Industrial Recovery Act which established a federal labor policy for interstate business. Because of its importance in the evolution of federal labor laws, section 7 (a) is here quoted in full:

Every code of fair competition, agreement, and license, approved, prescribed, or issued under this title shall contain the following conditions: (1) That employees shall have the right to organize and bargain collectively through representatives of their own choosing, and shall be free from the interference, restraint, or coercion of employers of labor, or their agents, in the designation of such representatives or in self-organization or in other concerted activities for the purpose of collective bargaining or other mutual aid or protection; (2) that no employee and no one seeking employment shall be required as a condition of employment to join any company union or to refrain from joining, organizing, or assisting a labor organization of his own choosing; and (3) that employers shall comply with the maximum hours of labor, minimum rates of pay, and other conditions of employment, approved or prescribed by the President.[1]

[1] 48 Stat. 198. The act was held unconstitutional in *Schechter Corp.* v. *United States,* 295 U. S. 495 (1935).

Section 7(a) was further supplemented by an amendment to the act on June 19, 1934. Under the amendment the President was authorized to establish boards "directed to investigate issues, facts, practices, or activities of employers or employees in any controversies arising under section 7a of said Act." A special function of the boards was "to order and conduct an election by a secret ballot of any of the employees of any employer, to determine by what person or persons or organization they desire to be represented in order to insure the right of employees to organize and to select their representatives for the purpose of collective bargaining as defined in section 7a of said Act and now incorporated herein."

The collective agreements which were embodied in the code were not necessarily made directly by the employers with their employees. In drafting the labor provisions incorporated in each code, it was customary for the representatives of the AFL to participate as negotiators. The collective agreements applied only to those industries in which codes of fair competition had been formulated and accepted and approved by the President. The collective bargaining principle, therefore, had a limited application; it did not apply to industries which had not organized to establish codes. Moreover, the labor provisions of the NIRA suffered from ineffective administration. Each industry had its own labor board, and there was no overall co-ordination establishing labor standards or even procedures. The amendments adopted in 1934 sought to correct some of the administrative defects, but the act was held unconstitutional by the Supreme Court in May 1935.

During the brief existence of the NRA from June 1933 to June 1935, the membership of the AFL had increased by 800,-000. In this two-year period, however, the AFL made little progress in unionizing the mass production industries, including automobiles, rubber, and textiles, nor did it make any headway in the distributive trades. Its membership growth occurred in those industries where unionism had previously gained some degree of organization.

LABOR'S BASIC CHARTER

The NRA demonstrated to labor leaders that federal intervention could be beneficial to organized labor, and they were loath to relinquish the gains achieved under the Recovery Act. As a result of experience with the NRA, the heads of trade unions had a change of heart and were now prepared to abandon the half-century traditional policy of self-help. When the National Industrial Recovery Act was declared unconstitutional by the Supreme Court, organized labor immediately sought the enactment of a law which not only embodied section 7 (a), but which also contained new features designed to strengthen the labor provision of that law. Labor achieved its goal in the enactment on July 5, 1935 of the National Labor Relations Act, commonly referred to as the Wagner Labor Act.

Future chapters will deal specifically and in detail with the many important aspects of the Wagner Act. Here we merely call attention to its general character as one step in the evolution of our federal labor policy. This law was a natural outgrowth of the labor provisions of the NIRA. The measure was promoted by organized labor and sponsored by members of Congress who were friendly to labor. The general philosophy of the act was stated in the Norris-LaGuardia Anti-Injunction Act, as well as in the National Industrial Recovery Act.

The expressed policy of the Wagner Act is based on two propositions: first, that the uninterrupted operation of interstate commerce would be furthered by strengthening the bargaining power of labor; and second, that our national economic welfare would be advanced and enhanced by the increased ability of labor to secure a larger share of the national income.

In pursuance of both of these objectives, the act encourages and promotes unionization and collective bargaining.

The NRA labor provisions applied only to those industries which voluntarily adopted codes of fair competition or industries which were licensed by the President. Under the NRA the labor sections were loosely administered. Many industries had their own labor boards. Until the act was amended in 1934, there was no co-ordination among the many industry boards. The Wagner Act has one central agency, the NLRB, which has exclusive jurisdiction in the administration of the act.

Whereas the NIRA lacked adequate enforcement provisions, the NLRA corrected this weakness. The NLRB can issue cease and desist orders against employers charged with violation of the law. These orders are enforceable by appeal to a Circuit Court of Appeals, and violation of its orders subjects the employer to contempt of court. Labor provisions of the NIRA were not specific in defining actions which were forbidden. The Wagner Act spells out in considerable detail the "unfair labor practices" on the part of an employer. It shall be an unfair labor practice for an employer:

(1) To interfere with, restrain, or coerce employees in the exercise of their rights to self-determination, to bargain through representatives of their own choosing, and to engage in concerted activities.

(2) To "dominate or interfere with the formation or administration of any labor organization, or contribute financial or other support to it." (The company-dominated union.)

(3) To enter into a closed-shop agreement with an employee organization in which only a minority of the employees are represented.

(4) To discharge or discriminate against an employee who files charges or gives testimony with respect to a complaint against the employer.

(5) To refuse to bargain with the representatives of his employees.

One of the primary functions of the NLRB is to designate bargaining units and to determine the proper representatives of those units. The administration of this function has had considerable influence in the selection of the bargaining representatives in plants and in industries.

The Wagner Act was frankly designed for the exclusive benefit of labor. The statute imposes no restrictions or obligations on labor. There is no such thing as an unfair practice by labor within the meaning of the act. The law imposes no restrictions on the right of labor to strike, picket, or boycott. It imposes no responsibility on unions with respect to violations of contracts which had been entered into as a result of the intervention of the NLRB. Nor does the act directly or indirectly regulate the internal organization of unions. Finally, although this act is to encourage and promote collective bargaining, the obligation to bargain collectively is not imposed on labor.

To understand the reason for the imposition of these restrictions and obligations on the employer, one must recall the period when the employer had the upper hand, and labor was the underdog. For many decades employers used their legal rights in an arbitrary and often unfair manner. Perhaps their own practices led the labor leaders to influence Congress to write into the law protection against the specific practices used by employers against unions. This may account for the pendulum swinging so far in favor of unions and against employers.

The Wagner Act provides no machinery or devices for the settlement of a labor dispute. The NLRB has no mediation or arbitral functions. The theory of the law is that controversies should be settled through the normal processes of collective bargaining. The proponents of the law hoped that strengthening and equalizing the bargaining power of labor would lead to peaceful settlement of disputes.

Organized labor was instrumental in securing the enactment of the Wagner Act. There was general opposition to it on the part of employers. After the act was passed, employers accepted it reluctantly and expected, or at least hoped, that the act would be declared unconstitutional. The Supreme Court upheld it in 1937.

The strength of unions has increased since the passing of this act. The total membership in all American labor unions was a little under 4 millions in 1935. Today the membership is estimated to be approximately 15 millions. It was under the administration of the Wagner Act that mass production industries became unionized. The union movement grew, therefore, not only in numbers but in the scope of its operations.

The stronger the unions became, the more influence they exerted in the selection of the personnel of the NLRB. This is especially important in view of the fact that the act gives to the Board very wide discretionary powers in the interpretation of the act. The AFL has felt aggrieved over the favoritism shown the CIO unions, especially in the matter of the selection of the bargaining unit.

INFLUENCE OF WORLD WAR II

During the war period, the Wagner Act remained in full force and effect. However, since the NLRB had no authority to deal with labor disputes, new machinery was created in the interest of the war effort. Many experiments were tried. The first step was the creation of the Office of Production Management headed by a joint directorship, Mr. Knudsen representing the employers, and Mr. Hillman representing labor. The machinery for handling combined production and labor problems worked badly. The work of the OPM was supplemented by the creation of the National Defense Mediation Board for facilitating the settlement of disputes in defense industries. The Mediation Board was composed of equal numbers of members of the AFL, the CIO, the employers, and the public. This machinery failed to function because it combined mediation and arbitration functions without having authority to enforce its arbitrational awards. It broke down on the question of the closed shop. An award refusing a closed shop in the captive coal mines caused the CIO members to withdraw from the Mediation Board.

The Mediation Board was succeeded by the National War Labor Board, created by executive order. For all practical purposes, this Board functioned on the theory of compulsory arbitration. While the Board had no legal authority to enforce its decisions, the President under the War Powers Act, could seize a plant and force a recalcitrant employer to accept the terms of the award. The chief executive, however, did not develop a comparable method for enforcing a decision of the Board against labor.

When strikes increased during the war, Congress stepped into the picture and passed the War Labor Disputes Act of 1943. This act prohibited the incitement or the encouragement to strike in government-operated plants or mines. Violations were punished by a fine of not to exceed $5,000, imprisonment of not more than one year, or both. In privately operated plants, the act called for a thirty-day cooling off period and the taking of a strike vote, supervised by the government. There was to be no interruption of production until after the strike had been voted on by a secret ballot. Employers could recover damages from unions for losses suffered through strikes called in violation of this act. In actual experience the act merely legalized strikes by providing a legal procedure before the walk-out.

The War Labor Board was deluged with cases in which such legalized strikes occurred. The outstanding defect in the operation of the WLB was that it had no body of principles on which to base its decisions. It considered each case on its merit, without the use of any predetermined yardstick. It is true that it adopted and used the Little Steel Formula, but the Board deviated so frequently from this formula that it could hardly be called a principle.

To the extent that the War Labor Board succeeded in keeping wages within bounds, it performed a valuable service in the general stabilization program during the war period. Prices would have got further out of control without the control of wages. This was demonstrated by events that followed the wage increase of 18½ cents per hour, granted in major industries after the Board passed out of existence. Shortly after V-J Day the War Labor Board was abolished, and in its place was created the Wage Stabilization Board. This Board has functioned very feebly. Wage controls were completely lifted on November 9, 1946.

CHAPTER II

SUMMARY OF THE LABOR POLICY OF THE FEDERAL GOVERNMENT

During the last fourteen years, the national government has sought by increasing the bargaining power of labor to enable employees to secure a larger income with shorter hours of work. There have been two other significant objectives in the labor policy of the government: first, it has attempted to protect the workers' right to organize in their own way; and second, it has endeavored to promote the peaceful settlement of labor disputes. Whenever these two secondary goals of the government clash with its efforts to increase bargaining power, the latter objective normally prevails over the other two.

By many separate pieces of legislation and through a multitude of administrative activities and decisions, the federal government has taken an active hand in shaping the course of industrial relations. An analysis of federal labor policy, however, reveals that the program as a whole is far from unified or consistent. There are cases where the policy set forth in one law or administered by one agency is inconsistent with that contained in other statutes or decisions. The principal reason for this lack of unity will be briefly discussed.

CONSTITUTIONAL DIFFICULTIES

The federal Constitution has been one of the major causes for the failure to develop a unified labor policy. There are two reasons for this: first, the national government is vested with only limited powers; and, second, our federal form of government has complicated the problem. Underlying the first of these sources of difficulty, is a fundamental principle of American constitutional law—that the national government can exercise only such powers as are necessary and proper to carry out the granted powers. The Constitution itself makes no direct grant of authority to the national government to regulate labor relations. Consequently, the federal government can act in this field only to the extent that it can use other delegated powers to attain such objectives. As a result, labor policy has sometimes been expressed indirectly and practically always in a fragmentary manner. From its power to regulate interstate commerce, the federal government derives its authority to control concerted activities of workers by such laws as the Sherman Antitrust Act or the Railway Labor Act. The power of Congress to control the jurisdiction and procedure of the federal courts is another source of authority. Through this approach Congress was able in the Norris-LaGuardia Act to make unenforceable in the federal courts any contract whereby an employee agreed not to join a union. Because the federal judiciary has jurisdiction of cases between parties who are citizens of different states and over cases involving the validity of state laws under the federal Constitution, the federal courts have been able to express views on the desirability and legality of picketing.

The second source of difficulty in developing a unified labor policy is our federal form of government. All powers not specifically granted to the national government belong to the states, unless the Constitution specifically denies them to the states. Hence, many problems of labor relations that the national government has not touched or cannot touch on are within the power of the states, should they care to exercise their authority. In many instances the federal government tacitly assumes that the states have exercised such authority in fields that are beyond the jurisdiction of the national government. Although the law has conferred upon workers a right to organize unions, the legal basis of such labor organizations at present springs entirely from state statute or common law. Again, employers have an obligation under national law to engage in collective bargaining, but the legal enforceability of the agreement arrived at by the collective bargaining process is generally determined by state law. Under federal law it may be legal for a trade union and an employer to enter into a closed-shop contract, but the right of a specific worker to join a union and the power of the union to expel him are determined not by the laws of the United States but by those of the several states.

Largely because of these constitutional limitations, the labor relations policy of the national government is embodied in many unrelated laws enacted at different times, to attain various objectives, and shaped by diverse forces. When a policy is embodied in many separate laws, inconsistencies and incongruities are almost inevitable. With this word of explanation, a brief summary of our present policy can be presented.

PRINCIPLES UNDERLYING GOVERNMENT POLICY

Promoting concerted action. To make it possible for employees to obtain better working conditions, the government has encouraged workers to engage in concerted action. The purpose of encouraging concerted action has been to help employees to make collective agreements with their employers. As a part of this program, efforts have been made to protect the right of the workers to engage in various forms of concerted action, including the organization of unions and the participation in strikes, picketing, and boycotts. The National Labor Relations Act and the Railway Labor Act have sought to accomplish this objective. Not only have employees been granted the right to organize, but the government actually encourages them to exercise that right on the premise that with an increase in union membership the bargaining power of employees will be augmented. In accordance with this idea, the National Labor Relations Board considers illegal any action of an employer that might discourage workers from organizing.

At present the right to strike is almost without limitation. Thus, employees cannot be discharged while they are on strike, and in a number of ways the government makes it difficult for an employer to operate his plant when the workers are on strike. For example, if an employer urges individual strikers to return to work, or if he employs strikebreakers, he commits an unfair labor practice under the National Labor Relations Act, and he must pay the wages of all strikers from the date he committed the unfair labor practice. Other forms of concerted action are also protected and encouraged. The Supreme Court has held that the workers have a constitutional right to picket, and this right has been construed broadly by the judiciary. The right to boycott is almost without limit. Finally, the legal responsibility and liability of trade unions are severely restricted.

Few limitations have been imposed on the workers' use of the various forms of concerted action. These instruments of self-help can be utilized even though the free movement of goods in interstate commerce is considerably limited thereby. Further, a minority group of employees with whom the employer is forbidden to bargain can strike in order to interfere with the legal rights of a majority union with which the employer must bargain. Under the National Labor Relations Act, when a majority of the employees has selected a bargaining representative, it is illegal for an employer to bargain with any other group of workers. Nevertheless, it is not illegal for minority groups of employees to use concerted action to coerce him to negotiate with them, although this would be an unfair labor practice prohibited by the National Labor Relations Act.

To stimulate the growth of union membership, and as a result, to increase union bargaining power, labor organizations except on railroads are encouraged to make various kinds of contracts that give preference to union members. Except on the railroads, closed-shop, union-shop, preferential-shop, and maintenance-of-membership agreements are all permitted when the negotiating union represents a majority of the employees.

To promote collective bargaining between employers and employees is the major objective of encouraging concerted action among workers. By federal statutes, workers are given the right to bargain collectively, and the law imposes on employers a corresponding duty to bargain with them. The nature of the employer's obligation to bargain collectively has been approached in different ways by various government agencies operating under different laws. Under the Railway Labor Act the obligation is fulfilled if the employer engages in certain procedures. The courts consider that it is immaterial whether those procedures actually result in an agreement.

Under the National Labor Relations Act, another test is used to determine whether the employer has engaged in collective bargaining. According to the decisions of the National Labor Relations Board, the real test of whether the employer bargained collectively is: Did the process of bargaining actually result in a collective agreement? If it did not, the Board attempts to discover whether the employer failed to grant those demands of his workers that the Board considers to be desirable, or whether the employer insisted upon the inclusion in the agreement of provisions that the Board considers to be undesirable. If the employer engaged in either of these activities, the Board has on a number of occasions found that he demonstrated bad faith in refusing to bargain collectively. Thus the Board has held that an employer demonstrated bad faith in bargaining if he insisted that both he and the union post a bond guaranteeing the specific performance of the contract or if he demanded that the union incorporate so that he could sue it for breach of contract. In several cases the Board has held that an employer failed to bargain if he refused to grant a closed shop when the union demanded it. As actually applied by the Board, these tests of what constitutes collective bargaining have been to the advantage of labor.

The negotiation of collective agreements is the final objective of the various types of concerted action that are being encouraged by the government. But some other aspects of the government's labor program actually tend to discourage employers from making such agreements. It is generally difficult for an employer effectively to enforce a collective agreement against a union and to recover damage suffered as a consequence of a breach of contract. Though a union contracts not to engage in strikes, picketing, or boycotts, it can nevertheless as a rule use with impunity such instruments of industrial warfare to compel the modification of the agreement or to attain any other objective. One of the major reasons an employer enters into an agreement with a union is to free his establishment from the interruptions resulting from activities such as strikes and boycotts. Many employers see little to be gained from a collective agreement if they are unable to secure this protection as a consequence.

Protecting the right of self-organization. The second of the three fundamental principles underlying the labor policy of the national government is that workers have a right to form their own organizations. To make this right a reality, employers are precluded from doing anything that interferes with the right of their workers to organize. The National Labor Relations Act offers a direct administrative remedy to enforce these rights, while the Railway Labor Act utilizes only criminal sanctions.

But the application of the right of self-organization involves a contradiction. If the employer is to know with which group of his employees he is required to bargain, some government agency must be empowered to determine the appropriate unit wherein bargaining is to take place, and it must be authorized also to discover which group of employees constitutes the majority in that unit. Since any government agency performing this function must in the long run actually select the bargaining unit, as a practical matter, the government agency cannot help but interfere with the free right of workers to choose their own form of labor organization. This is true because the composition of the bargaining unit is significant in determining what organization will be chosen to represent the majority of the employees in it; consequently, any government board or agency that determines the bargaining unit will inevitably have a great influence over the choice of the workers in selecting their bargaining representative. Demarcating the boundaries of a bargaining unit is as significant in determining the choice of the bargaining representative as is drawing the boundaries of a congressional district in determining the results of an election for a member of the House of Representatives.

The settlement of disputes. The third principle of the labor policy of the government is that the peaceful settlement of labor disputes should be encouraged. Various types of governmental machinery have been set up to mediate, investigate, and arbitrate industrial controversies. But in practically all instances where such machinery exists, the workers have a free right to choose whether they will use this machinery designed to facilitate a settlement without industrial warfare, or whether they will engage in a work stoppage to win their demands. In no case is the workers' right to strike really limited or restricted in order to encourage the use of such machinery for the peaceful settlement of disputes. But in some instances indirect sanctions are used to persuade employers to use these agencies.

The dominant emphasis upon bargaining power. The labor policy of the government involves the encouragement of workers to engage in concerted action, the protection of their right of self-organization, and the promotion of the peaceful settlement of labor disputes. As actually applied, these three objectives frequently conflict. When the desire of the government to increase the bargaining power of employees clashes with its efforts to protect their right of self-organization or with its program of encouraging the peaceful settlement of disputes, practically always the objective of increasing the bargaining power of workers prevails over the other two objectives. An attempt will be made to show that such conflicts exist and how they are generally resolved.

The efforts of the national government to encourage employees to engage in concerted action often come into conflict with its desire to promote the peaceful settlement of labor disputes. Though the government has set up agencies to protect the right of labor to organize and to bargain collectively, if workers feel that these rights have been infringed upon, they can use strikes, boycotts, or picketing at their own discretion, or on the other hand, they can call upon the appropriate government agency to help them to enforce their rights through the peaceful machinery provided by law. Nothing is done to make it more attractive for employees to use the machinery for the peaceful enforcement of these rights. If labor feels that its rights under a contract have been violated, it is free to engage in measures of self-help to enforce its own interpretation of the agreement, or it can seek to enforce it by an appropriate legal action in a court. But here again nothing is done to make the direct use of force unattractive to the workers.

If labor makes use of the United States Conciliation Service or of machinery designed to facilitate the peaceful settlement of disputes, it does not thereby place itself in a disadvantageous bargaining position. It loses little of the advantage it might attain through the use of direct action. The major objective of a conciliating agency is to avoid a work stoppage by almost any means that are not illegal. Consequently, in any proceeding before such an establishment, the party threatening to break the industrial peace has a definite advantage, because the conciliating agency tends to feel that the demands of the workers must be met if they are to be dissuaded from their threat to exercise their legal right to use measures of self-help that might disturb the industrial peace. Since almost any lock-out by employers is now illegal, most disputes involve strikes or the threat of strikes, and thus the workers are the party generally engaging in the direct threat to disturb the industrial peace. Though the workers might agree to conciliation, they are still free to strike if the proposed settlement should be unsatisfactory to them. This potentiality of the ultimate resort to a work stoppage tends to condition the terms of settlement proposed by a conciliator. Consequently, when labor submits a dispute to conciliation, it suffers no significant loss of bargaining power.

There is also an area of potential conflict between the policy of the government of protecting the workers' right of self-organization and its efforts to increase their bargaining power. Although all the workers have the right to organize, in any bargaining unit only that group that represents a majority of the employees has a right to bargain collectively. This principle of majority rule as established by the government tends to strengthen the bargaining power of the majority group of workers, because a union has just as much bargaining power as if it were chosen unanimously by the employees, although it represents only a bare majority of the workers. By the adoption of the majority principle, the bargaining power of the majority is increased, and the freedom of organization of the minority is diminished.

There are other illustrations of the manner in which clashes are resolved between the efforts of the government to increase bargaining power and its attempt to protect the workers' right of self-organization. Generally the larger the bargaining unit is the greater is the bargaining power of the workers in it; but when the size of the unit is increased, the right of individual employees to engage in self-organization is actually reduced. Groups of workers with specialized skills and problems can more effectively express their peculiar interests in small units than in large ones because of the greater likelihood that they will constitute a majority in a small unit. To guide the National Labor Relations Board in its task of selecting the appropriate unit, Congress has said that the Board should seek both to protect the workers' right to organize and to increase their bargaining power. Congress has left the Board with complete discretion to determine the relative weight that it desires to give to each of the objectives. But in applying these standards, the Board generally has considered that it is more important to increase the workers' bargaining power than to protect the right of self-organization of various groups of workers with specialized interests.

The concern of the National Labor Relations Board with the maximization of bargaining power rather than the protection of the workers' freedom of organization is also indicated by its attitude toward unaffiliated unions, in contrast to labor organizations affiliated with national organizations like the AFL or CIO. Obviously, a local union associated with a national organization will tend to have more bargaining power than an unaffiliated union, because the affiliated union can engage in concerted action on a wider plane (throughout a whole industry or a significant portion of it), and because it has greater resources at its disposal. The government in a number of ways tends to favor the development of unions affiliated with national organizations, and it attempts to discourage unaffiliated unions.

In practically all cases the difference in treatment accorded to affiliated unions, as compared with that accorded to non-affiliated unions, gives an advantage to the former. Thus, if an affiliated union is found to be employer-dominated, the National Labor Relations Board will permit it to appear on the ballot in a collective bargaining election, whereas an unaffiliated union that is found to be dominated in this manner cannot generally be selected as a bargaining representative by the workers. If an unaffiliated union has a closed-shop contract or a check-off agreement, this is considered to be evidence of employer domination; but that is not true if the organization receiving the preferential treatment is an affiliated union. If an employer has attempted to dominate an unaffiliated union, though all who have joined it assert that it is their real choice, the Board will disestablish it. If in a similar case the union involved is affiliated with a national organization, the Board requires only that the employer cease his attempts at domination. Here again, as a practical matter, the National Labor Relations Board places the attainment of increased bargaining power above the protection of the workers' right of self-organization.

The endorsement by the government of various forms of union-preference agreements tends to clash with its objective of protecting the workers' right of self-determination. If the only workers hired are already members of a given union, and if they are discharged when they cease to be members in good standing, it can hardly be said that the workers have the right to determine what union they wish to join. They are not completely free to select the union they wish to join, and obviously they cannot leave it when they see fit to do so. As a result of union-preference clauses in collective agreements, the bargaining power of the workers is augmented, both because of the resulting increase in the size of labor organizations and because the unions are thereby enabled to restrict the supply of labor. At the same time, however, the employees' right of self-organization is restricted.

CHAPTER III

POLITICAL ASPECTS OF THE LABOR MOVEMENT

In the preceding chapters we have traced the origin and outlined briefly the objectives of our federal labor policies. Federal statutes have successfully promoted concerted action and increased the bargaining power of labor. The inequality which once existed in respect to collective bargaining has been completely wiped out. But in its place a new inequality has been created. Labor is no longer the underdog in collective bargaining. Moreover, unions have come to wield tremendous political power. This new development has an impact on our political as well as our economic structure. The political implications of our labor policies and strategy will be examined in this chapter.

THE VOTING POWER OF LABOR

The magnitude of union membership is in itself some indication of the potential political power of unions. The total number of dues-paying members of all unions is approximately 15 millions. In its 1946 report, the AFL claims a membership of 7,151,808. The unofficial figure for the CIO is slightly more than 6 millions. The combined membership of the railroad and independent unions is close to 2 millions. While these 15 million unionists are not amalgamated into one organization, they have many common bonds.

It is not of course implied that all of the workers are of one mind politically or that union members can be delivered by their leaders to any political party or candidate. On the contrary, even so powerful a labor leader as John L. Lewis, whose word is law among coal miners on matters affecting union policy, was unable to switch any considerable number of votes away from Roosevelt to Willkie in the 1940 presidential campaign. The results, moreover, in the congressional elections of 1946 might cause the political leaders to revise their views with regard to the labor vote. While no detailed analysis has been made of the election returns, it would appear that even where the CIO–PAC operated, workers either abstained from voting or cast their ballots much like others in their respective communities. This was evidenced in such industrial states as New York, Pennsylvania, and Illinois.

Perhaps the party leaders will conclude that they have overestimated the ability of labor leaders to influence the rank and file. The secret ballot is cherished by workers who are members of unions; especially by members of unions that are operated on a nondemocratic basis, and where it is dangerous for individuals to oppose the union leaders in the open. Moreover, the lack of unity, due to the split between the AFL and the CIO, minimizes to some extent the use of the political weapon. The important fact, however, is that the leaders of our major political parties are fully aware of labor's potential voting strength, and consequently are careful to shape government decisions in line with the aspirations of labor.

In measuring the political influence of labor, we find that union membership is highly concentrated in industrial areas, and in many industrial states labor might well have the balance of power. The activities of the PAC in the 1946 congressional campaign were focused mainly in some fifteen states. Even in agricultural states there are local industrialized areas in which union labor has considerable influence. The political fortunes of congressional representatives in such manufacturing districts have been affected by the activities of labor in political campaigns.

INDUSTRY-WIDE STRIKES AND GOVERNMENT INTERVENTION

The high degree of control exercised by labor in some industries has produced a trend toward a new and more intense form of government intervention in the settlement of labor disputes. Almost complete unionization has been achieved in such important industries as coal, steel, automobile, rubber, meat-packing, construction, all forms of transportation, men's and women's wearing apparel, aluminum, agricultural implements, maritime and longshoring, newspaper printing, publishing, and aircraft. There are other important industries in which from 60 to 80 per cent of the employees are covered by collective bargaining agreements. These include electrical machinery and appliances, machinery and machine parts, petroleum refining, railroad equipment, rayon yarns, and woolens.

The tendency is more and more in the direction of industry-wide bargaining, as in the case of the soft-coal industry. In other industries—the electrical, steel, and automobile—wage contracts made with one or more major companies become the pattern for all the firms in the industry. This tendency is more noticeable in the mass production industries where the industrial type of union prevails. The forty national unions which make up the CIO partake of this character. The more than 100 national unions affiliated with the AFL are less adapted to industry-wide bargaining, but even with respect to the craft unions, there is a tendency to apply a national wage standard after making due allowance for differences in prevailing wages and cost of living in localities or regions. Where industry-wide bargaining does prevail, the heads of the national unions exercise tremendous political as well as economic power.

Because of the interdependence of industries in our present-day economy, an industry-wide strike in any key industry cripples production in other lines. The closing down of the mines in the soft-coal fields interferes with the production of steel and the running of steam railroads. A prolonged strike in the electrical field such as we have recently experienced, created a shortage of fractional horsepower motors essential to so many of our household appliances. Automobile production has been retarded because of strikes in plants which supply various parts to the automobile producer. The result is that we have cars without bumpers, upholstery, and other items. The recent prolonged strike in the maritime field has seriously interfered with the production and distribution of commodities in many lines.

When industry-wide strikes occur in key industries, the impact is felt throughout the economy. It affects the ability of companies in related industries to obtain essential materials; and it also affects the consuming public. The general public of course includes the labor population. The fact is that vast groups of workers often face involuntary unemployment as well as deprivation of essential consumption goods as a result of strikes in industries other than their own. This is what we have been witnessing for several years. When critical situations affecting the public interest develop, the federal government naturally becomes concerned and feels called upon to resolve the controversy.

Unions have come to expect federal intervention when an industry-wide strike affects the general public. In fact, this has become a part of union strategy. When there is a complete stoppage of the production of a basic commodity, the strike is in reality a strike against the general public, including workers indirectly affected, quite as much as it is a strike against the employers. In cases where the employer is the United States government, the strike or threat of strike is directly against the government itself. This was the situation in November 1946 in the coal industry.

COLLECTIVE BARGAINING AT THE WHITE HOUSE

Federal intervention has become so much a part of present strategy in the settlement of labor disputes that the influence of labor leaders is often measured by their ability to deal directly or indirectly with the White House or the President's advisers. Retention of power by labor leaders depends on their ability to secure gains for their union constituents. In this respect unions are not unlike political organizations. Labor leaders are in danger of being displaced if they fail to "deliver." Naturally labor leaders use their power in seeking the influence of political leaders when it is necessary or advantageous to do so. The political implications are obvious. In the settlement of economic problems, political expediency is likely to become the yardstick.[1]

On a number of occasions since 1933, the federal administration has shown solicitous regard for labor and the labor vote. The attitude of the government in the sit-down strike of 1937 is a case in point. Here was an unprecedented direct action on the part of the workers in the General Motors plants. The employees refused to work, but declined to leave the plants until the employers came to terms with them. The governor of Michigan, Frank Murphy, refused to take action looking to the eviction of the workers from the struck plants. The Secretary of Labor, Frances Perkins, took the position that it was her duty to seek a settlement of the dispute even while the sit-down strikers were still in the plants.[2] Her attitude was that until the courts passed on the legality of the sit-down strike, she would take no position against this drastic labor technique. The Department of Labor invited Mr. Sloan, head of General Motors, to come to Washington to confer concerning a settlement of the dispute. Mr. Sloan refused the invitation on the ground that to do so would be regarded as tacit approval of the sit-down strike. At a press conference President Roosevelt expressed disappointment at Mr. Sloan's refusal and said it was "unfortunate." Two years later, in 1939, the Supreme Court in the Fansteel case, ruled the sit-down strike illegal by holding that the strikers did not have the right to be reinstated in their former positions.[3]

[1] To illustrate, in the conference of October 1946 between John L. Lewis and President Truman's advisers with respect to the legal interpretations of the coal contract, the chairman of the Democratic National Committee was present at some of the meetings. *New York Times*, Oct. 30, 1946.

[2] In a recent book entitled, *The Roosevelt I Knew*, Mrs. Perkins states (p. 321), "Certainly the sit-down technique is unwise and demoralizing."

[3] *NLRB* v. *Fansteel Metallurgical Co.*, 306 U. S. 240 (1939).

In 1941, President Roosevelt interfered in a coal strike, in which the principal issue was the closed shop. There was machinery for deciding such an issue. The National Defense Mediation Board, composed of representatives of labor, employers, and the public had jurisdiction over such disputes. When this Board rendered a decision against the request of the union for a closed shop, the CIO members withdrew from the Board and thereby disrupted that agency. Following this decision, the President also took a stand against the closed shop—declaring at a press conference that "the Government of the United States will not order, nor will Congress pass legislation ordering, a so-called closed shop. . . . That would be too much like the Hitler methods toward labor." But the President did not adhere to this policy. When it was suggested that the dispute be submitted to arbitration, Mr. Lewis refused to agree. But when he subsequently learned that the President would appoint Mr. John Steelman as public member of the arbitration panel, he agreed to the proposal. Mr. Steelman decided in favor of Lewis, and the closed shop was granted.

Regardless of the merits of the case, this presidential interference demonstrated to unions with strong leadership that, by refusing to abide by awards of government boards, it could rely on gaining its point through White House intervention. This type of action naturally tends to destroy the prestige of such government agencies. The surrender to Lewis established a pattern which was followed by other strong unions. The path to the White House became an open road to political influence in the solution of our labor problems.

In the war period itself Mr. Lewis, when our men in the armed services were sacrificing their lives, did not refrain from again calling a strike. The situation became critical because production of essential munitions was dependent on the procurement of coal. The emergency was so great that President Roosevelt made a direct radio appeal to the miners to return to the pits, but they refused. Lewis's order, "No contract, no work," carried greater weight with his union members than the patriotic appeal of the Chief Executive. The miners did not go back to work until Mr. Lewis announced a fifteen-day truce and ordered them back to work. There was intermittent interruption in the production of coal for several months due to stoppages. During the months of April, May, and June of 1934, there was a loss of 6 million man-days in the coal industry. Again, the government capitulated and Lewis was victor.

This is the pattern which has been pursued down to the present. In October 1946 Lewis insisted on reopening the contract between the government and the United Mine Workers of America. At the strategic moment, only two weeks before the congressional elections, he warned the Secretary of the Interior, Mr. Krug, that the mines would be shut down on November 1 unless the government conferred with him by that date for the purpose of negotiating a new contract calling for changes in wages and working conditions.

Because of the emphasis we have placed on the activities of John L. Lewis, it might appear that we regard him as the cause of our recent labor troubles; we look upon him only as a symptom of the malady. A brilliant strategist and a daring leader, he simply took advantage of the weakness in our government labor policy and the inept handling by the government of disputes in which, unfortunately, political considerations commonly played a role of major importance.

It is often contended that White House intervention in industrial disputes is made necessary because no adequate machinery exists for their peaceful settlement. This argument falls to the ground when we consider what has occurred in the railroad transportation field. In 1926 Congress passed the Railway Labor Act which, with the 1934 amendments, has been held up as a model law for all management-labor relations. It will be recalled that the law was enacted at the joint request of the unions and railway management. Its primary objective was to get both parties to a dispute to settle their grievances by using the machinery of mediation, voluntary arbitration, or in emergencies, special fact-finding boards with power to make recommendations in the nature of awards.

Since 1941 the record is replete with examples of government intervention which has interfered with the normal operation of the Railway Labor Act, has seriously damaged the prestige of the National Mediation Board, and has raised doubts concerning the effectiveness of the act itself. In 1941 a dispute arose over the question of wages. When mediation failed and the unions rejected arbitration proposed by the carriers, the President appointed a five-man emergency board. The board made its findings and recommendations, which the carriers accepted. The railroad unions refused to accept the award. The union chiefs called on the President and urged him to intercede in order to get a more generous wage increase. The President acceded and appointed a new board which operated not merely as a fact-finding instrument but as a mediator as well. As a mediator, it persuaded the carriers to grant terms acceptable to the unions, with a tacit understanding that railroad rates would be increased.

Again, during a controversy in 1943–44, the machinery of the Railway Labor Act was badly mangled by undue government interference. An emergency board was headed by Professor I. L. Scharfman, a transportation authority regarded as sympathetic to labor. Judge Vinson, then Director of Stabilization, set aside the recommendation on the ground that it did not conform to the Little Steel Formula; and he requested that the Scharfman board reconvene and rehear the issues. The unions brought pressure on the Senate to legalize the wage increase, which the carriers agreed to pay, thus setting aside the application of the Stabilization Act as it might apply to railroads. Before the House acted on the Senate bill, the President appointed a new emergency board to re-examine the whole issue. The recommendations of this Board, headed by Judge Shaw, were rejected by the unions. In the meantime, the government took over the railroads. While the National Mediation Board was considering the dispute with some prospect of settlement, the President intervened. He proposed terms more favorable to the unions than they had originally demanded, and on the basis of his proposal a settlement was secured. It must be admitted that President Roosevelt averted railroad strikes; but his strategy in the handling of railroad cases discredited the Railway Labor Act and the machinery it had created; and the increased rates granted were at the expense of the public.

Other railroad labor disputes, based on wage demands, were settled by presidential intervention. In each instance labor rejected an award, and to avert a strike, the President took charge. In the final settlement in each case political consideration manifested itself in no uncertain manner. On one occasion, when an emergency board made its report to the President containing an award unanimously agreed upon by the unions and railway management, the President is reported to have asked in all seriousness how they came to agree on so low a figure. Obviously the President was playing to the union gallery for applause—and maybe votes.

The railroad strike in 1946, which plagued the Truman administration, was a direct result of the policy initiated by President Roosevelt and inherited by his successor. When the controversy in 1946 failed of adjustment, President Truman appointed a fact-finding board which made its findings. Most of the unions accepted the award, although reluctantly. The trainmen, however, rejected the findings, expecting President Truman to appoint another board as Mr. Roosevelt did in 1943. Their leaders threatened to strike unless their terms were met. The record is not clear, but there is some reason to believe that the labor leaders of the brotherhoods were hopeful that a compromise settlement would be made. In any case, a strike was called. President Truman was faced not only with a hostile union but an angry public. He appealed to the railroad workers to return to their jobs and addressed Congress regarding the dispute. The strike was broken.

President Truman was threatened with political retaliation by Mr. Whitney, president of the Brotherhood of Railroad Trainmen. Meanwhile Congress passed the Case bill, which the President vetoed, largely because organized labor was opposed to it. The Political Action Committee of the CIO announced it would oppose for re-election any member of Congress who voted for the Case bill, or who voted to override the President's veto of that bill.

Shortly after the defeat of Japan, labor began a concerted drive for substantial wage increases. Its objective was to maintain wartime earnings, including the time-and-a-half pay, though the hours of work might be shortened. The government supported this program on the ground that it was essential to the maintenance of over-all purchasing power and the prevention of deflation, accompanied by a substantial shrinkage in employment. This wage increase program was widespread, but the attention of the public was focused on several of our large mass production industries, including steel, automobiles, electrical machinery, meat packing, and petroleum.

The national administration threw its weight on the side of labor in its battle with employers to obtain a 30 per cent increase in rates. President Truman, in a radio address, told the American people that the workers were entitled to a substantial increase to preserve their take-home pay, adding that "industry as a whole can afford substantial wage increases without price increases." He did not go so far as to say that he favored a 30 per cent increase, but he did favor a substantial increase. Important government agencies supported the President's plea in championing labor's cause. The unions had claimed that the 30 per cent increase could be granted without necessitating an increase in prices. The Department of Commerce released a report supporting this proposal, stating that an increase of 20 to 25 per cent could be made in the automobile industry without a rise in prices. Secretary Wallace later (after the strikes were settled in the automobile and steel industries) admitted the report issued by his Department was in error and repudiated it. The contention of labor was also supported by Mr. Bowles, then head of OPA. Mr. Snyder, director of the Office of Mobilization and Reconversion, also supported this program for several months.

In an effort to settle the steel and automobile strikes, the President appointed fact-finding committees charged with responsibility for predetermining what level of wages these industries could pay in the difficult transition year 1946 without an increase in prices. The committees concluded that an increase of 18½ cents per hour without price increases was feasible. Meanwhile, without waiting for the report of the fact-finding committee, the President indicated he favored an 18½ per cent wage increase in the steel industry. The awards of the fact-finding bodies established a general pattern for all industries where organized labor was strong. The unorganized and hence weaker labor groups fared less well.

The question here at issue is whether it is sound public policy for the President and his subordinates to pronounce in advance what level of wage rates given industries can afford to pay. If their judgment as to the economic potentialities is faulty, the inevitable result is either a serious curtailment of production or advance in prices. How wide of the mark the judgment of the fact finders was is indicated by the fact that the OPA found it necessary within a few months to grant extensive compensating increases in prices, not only in steel and automobiles but more or less throughout the economy. It is our conclusion that no political agency, or no specially appointed fact-finding agency is in a position to determine what level of wages will prove to be possible, especially in a period of unstable conditions. Even if no political exigencies were involved, political agencies or fact-finding committees could not gauge with sufficient accuracy the complicated factors involved, either in the over-all business situation or in the conditions prevailing in particular industries, to warrant the setting of a wage-price relationship to be binding for months to come.

LABOR POLITICS IN ADMINISTRATION OF LABOR LAWS

The struggle for power between rival unions manifests itself in the administration of labor laws. Congress frequently lays down general policies and permits wide latitude to the administrators in the interpretation of the statutes. This is true, for example, of the Wagner Act. In the administration of that act, the NLRB was so constituted that it was partial to the industrial type of union in the selection of the bargaining unit. This favored the CIO, with the result that the AFL protested to the President that the craft unions were being discriminated against and brought a shake-up in the Board.

In a later case the Board permitted Henry Kaiser to sign a closed-shop agreement with the AFL union for workers in his shipyards at a time when only a handful of workers had as yet been hired. When the labor force in the yards grew to very large proportions (60,000 to 70,000), the AFL closed-shop agreement was continued despite the fact that large numbers of the workers preferred the CIO unions. The CIO demanded that the Board require an election to determine whether these yards should be CIO or AFL. The CIO charged that the Board was unfairly compelling a majority of the workers to join a minority union which was employer-dominated. Thus the political power of the CIO was pitted against the AFL on the question of whether the Board should modify its earlier stand. But in 1944 the AFL succeeded in getting an amendment to the appropriation bill for the NLRB which had the effect of forbidding consideration of any complaint in a case comparable to the Kaiser dispute.

On the other hand, there is a case in which the NLRB had designated the CIO as the exclusive bargaining unit for longshoremen on the Pacific Coast. Lumping all these workers into one bargaining unit did not meet with the approval of the AFL, since some of their locals controlled the situation in a few northern coast ports, situated on Puget Sound. The Federation had sufficient political influence to get the Board to modify its earlier decision so as to permit local AFL unions to be bargaining agents in a few ports where the CIO had no representation. Independent or unaffiliated unions of course would not have been treated with equal consideration.

Pressure by organized labor to secure a favorable interpretation of the Wagner Act is illustrated in the case of the unionization of foremen. The NLRB vacillated on this issue, but finally decided that the right of foremen to organize and bargain collectively did come within the meaning of the Wagner Act. At the same time, the Board imposed no restriction on the right of the foremen's union to affiliate either with the AFL or CIO. The complications that arose from this situation were numerous. In one case a foreman was found guilty of violating the Wagner Act by influencing workers to join a particular union. The question then became: Does the employer have a right to discharge the foreman? The NLRB refused the employer this authority. At this juncture we are not concerned with passing on the question of foremen's unions. We merely point out that organized labor had sufficient influence to get the NLRB to decide in favor of organized labor.

How deeply labor's political influence may extend is illustrated by another type of case. In 1944 the United Steelworkers of America, in efforts to secure a substantial wage increase, pressed for the elimination of the Little Steel Formula. The unions of the country attacked the accuracy of the government's cost-of-living index, constructed by the Bureau of Labor Statistics of the Department of Labor. Pressure was brought to bear against the Bureau's director, Mr. A. F. Hinrichs, acting commissioner, who insisted his index figure was as nearly correct as could be obtained. Two scientific organizations or groups assessed the work of the Bureau and found it substantially correct. Having failed to get Mr. Hinrichs to change his method of computing the index, the unions proceeded to use their political influence to get rid of him. He found his position uncomfortable and untenable and resigned. If there is any governmental activity that ought to be free from political influence, it is the function of such an agency, which gathers and disseminates economic data objectively and free from political pressure of any kind.

LABOR RESISTS CHANGES IN THE WAGNER ACT

Labor has had sufficient political power to prevent any important amendments to the Wagner Labor Act. It has lobbied against every change, and while several bills have passed the House, they have failed to pass the Senate. In 1946 Congress passed the Case bill amending the Wagner Act in several respects, but President Truman vetoed it, and his veto was sustained in the House.

The attitude of labor with respect to other federal labor laws is illustrated in its attack on the Hobbs Anti-Racketeering bill, which it vigorously opposed, but which finally passed both Houses and was signed by the President in 1946. The Anti-Racketeering Act makes unlawful the use of force, violence, or fear of injury to a person or his property in connection with the transportation of goods in interstate commerce. It was directed more specifically against the extortion practices by members of the teamsters' union. These actions were declared by the Supreme Court as not coming within the meaning of the Byrnes Anti-Racketeering Act of 1934. The act of 1946 does not in any way deprive the unions of rights to engage in legal activities. It is true, however, that the act does deprive the unions of the right to do those things which, when done by others, are regarded as unlawful. Though the Hobbs bill received substantial endorsement in both branches of Congress and was signed by the President, members of Congress who voted in the affirmative have been branded by the CIO-PAC as unfriendly to organized labor and threatened with political retaliation.

The attitude of organized labor was again demonstrated in its effort to defeat the Lea bill which sought to outlaw certain union activities affecting unfavorably radio broadcasting and the making of recordings. This congressional action was deemed to be necessary because the practices of the American Federation of Musicians, of which Mr. Petrillo was president, were declared by the Supreme Court exempt from our anti-trust laws. The bill had for its purpose the outlawing of unreasonable restrictions imposed by Mr. Petrillo and his union. The bill was enacted and approved by the President on April 16, 1946. The constitutionality of the act is now being contested. Mr. Petrillo and his union are represented in this case by Mr. Padway, who is also general counsel for the AFL.

THE INFLUENCE OF LABOR IN NONENFORCEMENT OF LAWS

It is not only in the federal field that the political power of labor manifests itself. In industrial communities where the labor vote is an important factor in elections, it is with great reluctance that the elected officials of a community will take any action that interferes with activities carried on by organized labor in time of a strike. State, county, and municipal officials are timid in breaking up mass picketing, though it interferes with the exercise of legal, normal rights of the public. Numerous cases could be cited where such absence of law enforcement has occurred. The most recent case is that of the strike of public utility workers in the Pittsburgh area, which resulted in a tie-up of a large portion of the economic life of the community. The strike directly affected only a little more than a thousand workers, but the net effect was to displace workers running into more than 50,000, and to shut-down factories, street railways, and department stores.

The recent strike of truckers in the Greater New York area is still another case in which the law enforcement officers refused to interfere with the activities of the strikers, even when those activities paralyzed a considerable segment of the economy, including of course innocent third parties. In the state of Connecticut an employer was denied entrance into or exit from his plant by virtue of mass picketing. An appeal to the governor and the local police brought him no relief. Cases of this type could be multiplied, and they have occurred in all parts of our country.

Economic blocs possessing political power are not new in our political history. We have had experience with other blocs: manufacturers, railroad interests, financial groups, and farmers. No one in these groups has ever laid claim to the voting strength now in the hands of organized labor. Business interest groups, however, achieve political influence through large financial contributions to political parties. Though the methods of achieving control differ, the results are similar. Each group uses its political power to secure the enactment of laws for its special interest; and each group clings tenaciously to its special privileges and resists changes in the law. The labor group is no exception to this long-recognized practice.

In a recent address delivered at the Steelworkers Convention, Philip Murray, president of the CIO, is reported to have made the following statement: "The destinies of the people of the United States and the destinies of this nation are . . . in the hands of American labor."[4] It is one of the principal obligations of our federal government to make certain that no single group in our economy is permitted to dominate national

[4] *Proceedings of the Third Constitutional Convention of the United Steelworkers of America,* May 14–18, 1946, p. 261.

policy. To achieve the maximum public welfare, it is essential that our government preserve a proper balance among conflicting economic interests.

In his final public address, the late Joseph B. Eastman, chairman of the Interstate Commerce Commission and director of the Office of Defense Transportation, declared:[5] "I can well remember the time when it was a dangerous thing to incur the displeasure of bankers, but there has been no danger in this since 1932. It became a greater danger to incur the displeasure of farm or labor organizations."

[5] At a banquet at the Hotel Statler, Feb. 17, 1946.

PART II

NATIONAL GOALS AND REQUIREMENTS

In preceding chapters we traced the evolution of the labor movement in the United States and the development of the labor policies of the federal government. It was shown that the central purpose of national labor policy has been to extend and strengthen in every possible way the bargaining power of labor, without adequate consideration of the effects on the nation as a whole. We have seen that the result has been to place labor and labor leaders in a position of dominant economic and political importance; and that the settlement of almost all major disputes has, in recent years, been transferred from the realm of private negotiation to the arena of national politics.

In determining what steps the government should take to modify its present policy, it is desirable to take a fresh look at the entire labor problem. Decisions as to labor policy should not be made solely on the basis of possible benefit to a single group in the body politic. The problem must be approached from the viewpoint of the national interest as a whole.

In chapters IV and V, we shall present in general terms the essentials of public interest in the problem of labor relations. It will, we assume, be generally agreed that the national labor policy ought to be designed to promote the major objectives or goals of our society. Therefore, these goals so far as they relate to the problem, will be summarized in chapter IV. In the succeeding one there will be discussed some of the major underlying considerations that should constitute the basis of national policy for labor. The relationship of the more important of these goals of society to the underlying considerations will be pointed out. The special problems involved in the various aspects of the national labor policy will be developed in Part III.

CHAPTER IV

BASIC NATIONAL GOALS AND CONCEPTIONS

There is probably more widespread agreement than is generally realized with respect to the basic economic, political, and social goals and objectives of the community. Most of the apparent disagreement on questions of national interest arises from differences concerning the means of attaining these goals rather than the desirability of the basic objectives themselves. The major goals of our society that bear on the problem of labor policy will be presented briefly.

An ever-expanding national income. It is universally agreed that a progressively larger total national income is one of our major economic objectives. Almost every individual member of the community desires a greater income in order to attain a higher standard of living. The aggregate national product is far from adequate to satisfy all of the potential needs of the American people.

The desirability of a higher standard of living is emphasized by the oft-repeated statement that one third of the nation is ill-fed, ill-housed, and ill-clothed. There is ample factual evidence to sustain the validity of this slogan. Government studies show that in 1941–42 a very large segment of the population did not have income sufficient to satisfy its primary wants. At that time the average income of all families in the United States was $1,540. Forty-seven per cent of the families actually received less than $1,500 a year, and income was under $1,000 for 32 per cent. One hardly needs to cite elaborate statistics to prove that the average family of 3.8 persons was not able to satisfy all of its wants on an income of $1,000 a year at the prices then existing. It is significant that in that year the average consuming unit with an income of less than $1,000 spent for current needs $100 in excess of its current income. The Bureau of Labor Statistics estimated that in 1942 the average family required at least $1,600 to meet its minimum needs on a "subsistence level"; but at that time the income of over 50 per cent of all families was less than that. Another source estimated that, to maintain a level of health and decency, the average family required $2,060 a year; but 61 per cent of all families had incomes of less than $2,000 a year.

The need for increasing the national income is apparent from the evidence concerning the actual earnings received by families and the amount of money required to sustain a minimum level of living. It is not always recognized, however, that the attainment of a higher and more desirable standard of living is dependent on increasing our real national income— that is, the sum total of all goods and services available for consumption.

Progressively wider distribution of income. A generally accepted economic objective is the attainment of a progressively wider division of the national income. In most cases larger incomes for workers and producers make for an increase in industrial efficiency, because with increased incomes workers can maintain a better standard of health and a happier state of mind. A wider distribution of income is essential for the continued economic growth of society as a whole, because the expansion of production involved in an ever-increasing national production requires a corresponding expansion of markets, and this in turn is dependent on constantly increasing buying power among the masses of human beings whose wants constitute the ultimate basis for economic activity. Moreover, only a broadening distribution of income is consistent with the basic conceptions of democracy.

Reduced effort in production. Another basic objective of our society is to reduce the amount of human effort required to produce a given quantity of goods or services. At the very time the community desires an ever-increasing national income, it also seeks a shorter work week. That is, we wish simultaneously to enjoy more goods and more leisure. Since productivity is restricted, we compromise between these conflicting desires. As technological progress occurs, society takes the benefits in part in a greater volume of goods and in part in greater leisure. For example, between 1900 and 1930 per capita production for the American economy as a whole increased about 40 per cent, while the work week was reduced approximately 13 per cent.

Reward based on effort. Most people wish to have an individual rewarded primarily on the basis of the work he actually has done. It is felt that the individual worker should be paid for the work he really does, and that his remuneration should not be based primarily on his needs. The obvious objective is to promote efficiency. This means that the national labor policy should make possible a system of wage payments based upon what the individual worker produces. Differentials in the rate of pay should exist where differences in skill exist, and wages should be closely related to the productivity both of the worker and of the enterprise where he is employed. A desirable labor policy should be designed to promote methods of wage payment that will attain these objectives.

Full development of individual capacities. It is widely assumed that society must make possible the largest opportunity for the development of the capacity of every individual in the community, and that it should facilitate the full utilization of his capacities. Stimulating the full development of the individual is, indeed, the basic preconception of democracy, the primary object of which is the full development of the individual, mainly through his own efforts. The application of the intelligence of each individual means advancement both for him and for the entire economy. Through the development of the individual's capacities, society as a whole progresses and the individual's happiness and material well-being are promoted. By contrast, the stultification of the members of the group would mean the general deterioration of the society as a whole.

There should be no barriers to hinder individuals in developing their capacities. The employee should not be restricted from using his full capacities to the greatest extent he wishes, except when this might affect the health and safety of the entire group. It is also generally believed to be desirable that an individual should have the free right to shift from job to job and shift employment from one locality to another, if he believes that this would be to his advantage.

Right of association. One of the major political and social conceptions of our society is that like-minded individuals should have a free right to form associations to accomplish common objectives—provided such association does not interfere with the equal rights of others. There is also a comparable right —that each individual is free to refrain from joining any and all associations if he so desires. On this assumption workers have the obvious right to join or not to join labor associations.

Avoidance of violence. The suppression of force and violence as a means of enforcing private rights is a universally accepted tenet of our society. Even where no adequate legal remedy exists for an alleged wrong, the use of private force as a method of enforcing rights is forbidden. The use of force as a means of self-help is generally prohibited except where it is absolutely necessary for self-protection. There are two reasons for the opposition to violence: first, justice, not brute force, should be the basis for adjusting differences; and second, the safety of innocent third parties is endangered by the use of violence by persons attempting to enforce their own rights.

Free speech. Freedom of speech is a prerequisite of democracy. Only through free expression and discussion can error be exposed, truth developed, and progress furthered. It is for the national good that freedom of speech is guaranteed all members of the society. Individuals are, however, held accountable for abuses of this right.

This is not an exhaustive catalogue of the goals and conceptions of our society. We have presented only those that are directly related to the development of national labor policy.

CHAPTER V

UNDERLYING CONSIDERATIONS IN NATIONAL LABOR POLICY

Underlying many of the special problems which make up the national labor program as a whole are a few general considerations of major significance. Since these underlying considerations cut across the many specific labor problems that are to be considered in later chapters, it seems desirable to discuss them in advance.

The analysis will be facilitated by organizing the discussion around a series of positive statements

1. Labor unions perform a necessary function.

2. Restrictive labor practices are undesirable.

3. Collective bargaining should be between employers and workers in specific companies.

4. Labor conflicts should not be extended to injure innocent third parties.

5. The peaceful settlement of industrial disputes should be facilitated.

An attempt will be made to show how the national policy relative to labor should rest on these basic considerations, and that these major elements are dictated by the goals considered in the preceding chapter.

LABOR UNIONS PERFORM A NECESSARY FUNCTION

From the standpoint of the major conceptions and objectives of our society, a desirable national labor policy should permit the employees to organize labor unions and to engage in concerted action for the purposes of collective bargaining. Under present conditions this involves some governmental protection in the exercise of that right by labor. The protection of the right is justified for two reasons.

The first argument is that individuals have an acknowledged right to form associations, and that such right merits protection when its exercise is actively interfered with. The right of association is desirable, because it facilitates the full development of the individual personality. It makes possible the interchange of information, the development of ideas, and the execution of common objectives. It is immaterial whether the objective is social, intellectual, fraternal, religious, business, or labor relations, individuals have a right to associate with other like-minded persons. No one may interfere with the right of association, irrespective of its objective (provided that it is not illegal). In most cases this right has never been questioned, because no one thinks of trespassing it. But since employers in the past have strenuously opposed the organization of unions, the question of government protection is important.

Second, on economic grounds there is a positive argument for the protection of the workers' right to form unions and to use concerted action. Labor organizations and the use of concerted action are, within limits, important devices for attaining some economic objectives. As previously pointed out, a steadily increasing national income is universally desired. To attain this objective, a progressively wider distribution of income is necessary to ensure that there will be an effective demand to take off the market the additional goods produced. If a great part of the national income is concentrated in the hands of a few who have a limited capacity to consume, while the great mass of people do not have even sufficient income to satisfy their basic wants, the market will not absorb the goods resulting from the increased production that is required to bring about rise in the standard of living. A wider market can be obtained only by narrowing the gap between the money wages paid to workers and the prices they pay for the goods they consume. In an economy where workers are paid in money, this narrowing of the gap can be attained by increasing wages relative to prices or by reducing prices relative to wages.

Since the beginning of the nineteenth century, the distribution of the expanding real income of society has been attained chiefly through increases in money wages relative to prices. But the most rapid increase in the real income of fully employed workers has taken place in periods of depression when prices fell more rapidly than wage rates; of course it was only after employment had picked up in the next upswing of the business cycle that the wage earners generally derived the full benefit from the decline in prices that occurred in the depression.

Because it has been primarily through increases in wage rates as compared with prices that the wider spread between earnings and prices has been effected, it appears that unions are a most significant device for bringing about a wider distribution of income. This is because there have always been forces operating in a competitive society which tend to keep wages lower than the existing state of productivity warrants.

Since labor costs constitute a very large item in the total cost of production of most manufactured or processed goods, every producer is under pressure to reduce costs by cutting wages, thereby gaining an advantage over his competitors.[1] Even though the consequences of such a wage reduction might be undesirable for the economy as a whole, it is to the advantage of the individual employer to cut wages if he can. Thus unions, which have resisted wage cutting and constantly negotiated for higher rates, perform a definite economic function in our society. Only through organization can workers attain a bargaining power commensurate with that of their employer. Unions tend to counteract the forces that depress wages. Thereby they facilitate the wider distribution of the national income, which is one of our major goals.

In considering unions as a means of narrowing the spread between wages and prices, it should be remembered that there

[1] In the calendar year 1945, wages and salaries represented 68 per cent of the total national income.

are limitations on attaining this objective, primarily through increases in money wage rates. An increase in the wage rate generally means an increase in costs, and higher costs tend to produce higher prices unless the increased wages are accompanied by a comparable increase in labor productivity. Such higher prices would work against narrowing the gap between wages and prices that might result from the wage increases. Moreover, since any group of employees consumes only a small fraction of the goods that they themselves produce, an increase in the wages of that group will not necessarily generate an increase in the demand for the specific goods produced by them. An increase in money wages would stimulate an increase in general demand only if the wage increase occurred simultaneously through the whole economy. Despite these limitations, unions have served a useful economic function in bringing about an improved ratio between wages and prices.

RESTRICTIVE LABOR PRACTICES ARE UNDESIRABLE

The attainment of increased production with reduced human effort is a most significant goal of our society. Any practices of employers, workers, or other groups that tend to restrict production and limit efficiency are highly undesirable. Such practices on the part of employers are forbidden by our anti-trust law; but the law does not prohibit unions from engaging in similar restrictive practices. Since this study deals with labor policy, however, only the practices of workers that reduce efficiency will be considered. The need for increased production and higher labor efficiency will be analyzed. Following the analysis, some illustrations of practices of organized labor that impede its attainment will be presented.

To attain a higher standard of living requires the production of more goods and services for consumption. While people desire an increasing standard of living, they are also anxious to reduce the amount of human effort required in production. This is another of our major goals. An increase in output per man-hour can be accomplished in two ways: by improving machinery, which increases the producing capacity of the individual who operates the machine; and second, by better performance on the part of the individual workman. It is with the latter phase of this problem that we are here directly concerned. While historically the improvement in machinery (technological progress) has been of primary importance in increasing man-hour output and in raising standards of living, the second factor, namely, the performance of individual workers, should not be regarded as of minor significance. By virtue of its numerical importance, labor still remains a fundamental factor in production, and upon the performance of workers depends in no small degree the efficiency of the machine itself.

Not infrequently concerted action is utilized by organized labor to restrict production. Fear of unemployment resulting from overproduction is the main reason for such practices. The activities of organized workers have brought about two major types of restrictive labor practices: first, are those that are avowedly of a make-work nature, and second, are those that are a consequence of the insistence upon using old methods of production, although technological changes have resulted in more efficient ways of doing the work. Make-work practices of the first type include the employment of unnecessary workers, the direct limitation of output, and the flagrant requirement that work be done twice. Each of these will be illustrated.

There are many instances where labor organizations require the employment of unnecessary workers. Thus the Brotherhood of Locomotive Firemen and Enginemen continues to require the employment of firemen on diesel engines where there is no fire to tend. In some states, railway labor has secured the adoption of so-called full-train-crew laws that necessitate the use of a given number of workers on a train, irrespective of its actual needs. Frequently the Musicians' Union demands the employment of more musicians in orchestras than are necessary. Motion picture operators insist upon the employment of unnecessary workers in projection booths.

The direct limitation of the output of workers is practiced by some labor organizations. The Lathers' Union has limited the amount of lathing that its members are permitted to install in a day. Linotype operators have restricted the amount of type that can be set. Painters prohibit the use of wide brushes. The United Automobile Workers of America stated on one occasion that one of its avowed objectives was to reduce man-hour output in the automobile industry.[2]

In some instances labor organizations have insisted that work be done twice. A local of the International Brotherhood of Electrical Workers in New York City requires that switchboards and generators manufactured by employees who do not belong to that union must be rewired by its members before they will install them. Plumbers demand that pipe be threaded on the job and not in the shop. Where pipe has been threaded in a shop they require that it be rethreaded on the job.

Unions not infrequently have fought the introduction of technological improvements because of fear that as a result of their use less labor would be required. In some cases this opposition has been carried on despite disastrous results to the employees' organization itself. The opposition of the Cigar Makers Union to the introduction of machinery for the manufacture of cigars resulted in a 50 per cent decline in its membership during a period of eleven years, although the total number of employees in the industry increased by 10 per cent.

Labor justifies these inefficient practices, because it fears over-production. Actually this fear is not well founded. During the past century, the demand for goods has steadily increased, while the amount of labor required per unit of output has declined. There has always been a great unfilled demand for goods, especially when the products are available at low prices. As has been said previously, a very large proportion

[2] TNEC Hearings, Vol. 30, p. 16375.

of the population is not able to buy all the goods necessary to maintain a minimum standard of living. The size of the unfilled demand, existing because low-income families are unable to satisfy all their wants at current prices, is such as to dispel any fear that overproduction would be a long-run result of increased labor efficiency, accompanied by lower prices.

Since increased production with reduced exertion is so desirable, national labor policy should positively promote this objective and oppose activities that are inconsistent with it. It may be asked: If this goal is so evident, cannot the leaders of organized labor be trusted to promote it by their own efforts? One obvious answer is, they have not done so. Another is that the short-term advantage of small groups of workers can be furthered by practices that conflict with the long-term interests of those workers and of the community.

COLLECTIVE BARGAINING SHOULD BE BETWEEN AN EMPLOYER AND HIS EMPLOYEES

Another fundamental of national labor policy is that collective bargaining ought to be carried on between a given employer and his own employees, and not between a group of employers and their workers. This element is basic because it is necessary to promote increased efficiency.

Collective bargaining has, for natural reasons, been tending steadily toward industry-wide bargaining. Workers desire to have the unit include not only all employers that may be potential competitors for labor but also all those who are likely to be competitors for markets for their products. Labor is anxious to extend the bargaining unit so as to embrace all producers that may be able to compete on the basis of wages. And in a country with nation-wide markets, this frequently means industry-wide bargaining because each producer is a potential competitor for markets with every other producer.

Efficiency in our present economy can best be measured on the basis of the operation of an individual company or plant.

The increased productivity of labor warrants increased remuneration, but an increase in productivity in a particular company cannot be made the basis for an increase in wages in competing companies which have no increase in efficiency. Effective systems for rewarding or stimulating labor efficiency can only be applied to individual plants or enterprises. Some of the gains resulting from increased efficiency must be distributed to labor as well as to the owners of capital to stimulate further efforts to increased efficiency. At the same time a large portion must go to the consumer in the form of lower prices in order to stimulate increased demand. Such an allocation of technological gains can be made only on the basis of the company that makes the gains, for it has to market its own product and attract necessary labor and capital. As a general consequence, one basic principle of a sound labor policy is that collective bargaining should be between a single employer and the representatives of his employees.

If in an industry-wide collective agreement wages were fixed at a level that the least efficient could afford, they would be lower than the more efficient can pay. On the other hand, if the production of the more efficient plants were used as the determining factor, the least efficient ones could not afford the wages and would be driven out of business. In practice, the bargaining power of labor is now such that wages set by industry-wide action will more frequently be closer to what the most efficient can afford than to what the least efficient are able to pay. Thus, to make it possible to keep the less efficient firms in business, some form of price fixing becomes inevitable. Prices thus fixed will be higher than would prevail under free competition. This would be detrimental to the consuming public.

Industry-wide bargaining, as pointed out in Chapter III, tends to result in the political determination of the conditions of employment. When labor organizes an entire industry, it can through strikes shut off practically the entire production of a given commodity. In a highly integrated economy, a national stoppage of production has grave repercussions on society. Industrial interdependence is the rule rather than the exception. As a result of a strike in one industry, the production of many related products in other industries is slowed down or completely stopped. The absence of one service or product can frequently tie up the production of many other goods. Inevitably the government intervenes in such a dispute, because the operation of the entire economic system may be jeopardized.

Settlements arranged through such governmental intervention are not based primarily on the economic considerations involved. The terms are not designed to stimulate efficiency. The primary consideration of the government often has been: What is necessary in order to avert or terminate the disruption of production? Peace at any price very often is a costly peace. The government frequently desires a solution that will be politically pleasing to the workers. The political power of organized labor is not discounted by administrators and politicians. The potential votes of the workers are not overlooked. This means that their demands commonly are given special consideration. The interests of employers and consumers are not as pressing politically as are those of the workers. Labor is enabled to secure wage increases not related to productive efficiency. The employees frequently are in a position to secure for themselves most of the fruits of technological change, thus leaving none to be distributed to owners of capital and to consumers in the form of lower prices. Railroads are a notable example.

It should also be noted that industry-wide bargaining as it now exists gives a monopolistic position to labor organizations. This results from the fact that the law permits unions to take disciplinary measures to enforce decisions upon their members. Concerted action on the part of employers in shutting down or limiting production would properly be regarded as a violation of the antitrust laws. If one were to attempt to make the bargaining power of employers equal to that of employees, it would seem that employers should also be permitted to form trade associations with disciplinary powers over their members. For instance, the employers' association would have to be empowered to penalize any member who signed a collective agreement with terms at variance with those prescribed by the association. The employers' association would need to have the power to close down the plants of its members if it were unable to get the union to accept the terms proposed. Such a monopolistic employers' association would of course be regarded as fundamentally opposed to the public interest.

LABOR CONFLICTS SHOULD NOT BE EXTENDED TO INJURE INNOCENT THIRD PARTIES

Over many centuries Anglo-American law has sought to limit the areas in which private warfare is permitted. Even where no legal remedy exists for a wrong, force and violence are not regarded as proper means of securing satisfaction. Private warfare involves the possibility of injury to innocent third persons, who are in no way parties to the dispute, and also to society as a whole. Only in the field of industrial relations is private warfare permitted. In labor disputes, law enforcement officers tolerate violence that would not be permitted in a comparable situation.

This is not the place to discuss all the ways in which industrial conflicts affect innocent third parties or to suggest appropriate remedies. Some illustrations will, however, serve to clarify the nature of the problem. One example is the sympathetic strike. Here workers strike in sympathy with other groups of workers, though they have no grievance against their own employers. Such activities have adverse effects upon their employers, who are innocent of any wrongdoing, and by maximizing the pressure of the strikers in the original dispute, the general public is also adversely affected.

Another example is the boycott. This involves the refusal by a group of workers to process or handle material because of certain conditions that existed when the goods were produced, processed, or handled by other groups of employees. The boycott has the effect of spreading industrial warfare to groups of workers who have nothing to gain for themselves by a disruption of production that may possibly injure the entire community.

Jurisdictional strikes constitute another illustration of concerted action that involves injury to a third party. Such disputes consist of a refusal to work by one union because an employer bargained with a rival organization, or because he gave specific tasks to members of a competing union. In most cases if the employer reversed his decision to satisfy the strikers, the other union would strike. There is nothing the employer can do to save himself from injury. He is not a party to the controversy; the dispute is between two rival unions struggling for jurisdiction and power.

Industry-wide bargaining also tends to extend the scope of the injury to innocent third parties. Where a collective agreement applies to two or more employers, the breach of it by any one of them provokes the workers to take concerted action against all of them. Injury is done to employers with whom the workers have no quarrel and who can do nothing to remedy the situation. It also involves injury to the general consuming public by a complete cessation of production of a necessary product.

MACHINERY SHOULD EXIST TO ENCOURAGE THE PEACEFUL SETTLEMENT OF DISPUTES

The peaceful settlement of disputes is another basic element of a desirable national labor policy. Work stoppages interfere with production; therefore it is desirable to facilitate the settlement of disputes before they result in stoppages. Because industrial warfare involves the potentiality of injury to the public and to innocent third parties, the use of peaceful remedies for the settlement of disputes should be encouraged. Unless one believes that the government should prescribe all conditions of employment and completely prohibit strikes, some disputes, especially those involving questions of interest, inevitably will involve a trial of strength between the parties.

To meet such situations, it is desirable that the government attempt to bring the parties together so that they can at least bargain about the questions involved. If the parties continue to fight it out without even discussing the matter, the dispute is prolonged unnecessarily, to the public injury.

It is advantageous to have machinery that will ensure that the parties will settle their difficulties with a minimum of public inconvenience and disturbance. This does not mean that it is appropriate for the government to substitute its ideas of a proper solution for those of either or both parties, where the dispute does not involve the mere interpretation of an existing agreement. The government should merely help to bring the parties together to facilitate a rapid settlement, and it should perform this function in a completely impartial manner.

PART III

A NATIONAL LABOR POLICY

In Part III we shall develop concrete recommendations for the improvement of national labor policy. If these suggested modifications are adopted, it is believed that the labor program will promote the goals and underlying considerations that were discussed in Part II. Before definite suggestions for changing our present policy can be presented, we must examine the policy of the government on specific subjects, as they are embodied both in the laws and their application. The attitude and practice of the government will be analyzed and appraised in the light of our goals and underlying considerations, and after this has been done, the specific suggestions for modification will be presented.

In Chapter VI the policy of the government toward the right to organize will be examined. We shall consider the question, Should the government merely protect the right to organize, or should it actually encourage the formation of unions? Workers form unions for the purpose of engaging in concerted action to attain collective agreements fixing the conditions of employment. The primary weapons used by labor organizations in this process are strikes, picketing, and boycotts. What the attitude of the government should be toward these implements of industrial warfare will be considered in Chapter VII. The nature of the obligation to bargain collectively and the rights and duties arising out of the resulting collective agreement will be the subject of Chapter VIII.

If workers are to have the right to bargain collectively, some government agency must determine the specific groups of employees with which an employer must bargain. The designation of the bargaining unit by the government will be examined in Chapter IX. The relationship of the individual employees to their labor organizations will be considered in Chapter X.

67

The administrative machinery for enforcing the basic rights and duties of employers and employees in the field of industrial relations will be examined in Chapter XI. What the government does to facilitate the peaceful settlement of labor disputes will be investigated in Chapter XII. Steps that should be taken to promote the peaceful adjustment of industrial controversies will be presented in Chapter XIII.

CHAPTER VI

THE RIGHT TO ORGANIZE

How far should the government go in protecting employees when they seek to organize? Should it actively promote unions? Is it desirable for the state to permit employers and employees to agree to give special advantages to union members?

PROTECTING THE RIGHT TO ORGANIZE

By the Railway Labor Act and the National Labor Relations Act, the government protects the right of workers to organize. But as actually administered and interpreted, the NLRA has been changed so that it is now used as a means of positively promoting labor organizations. For this reason, more detailed consideration will have to be given to the National Labor Relations Act than to the Railway Labor Act. The interpretation that the National Labor Relations Board and the courts have given to the law will be summarized, and then the significance of the law as thus interpreted will be considered.[1]

Railway Labor Act. The Railway Labor Act of 1926 as amended in 1934 makes it a misdemeanor for employers subject to its terms to do the following things: (1) to interfere with the free right of their employees to choose representatives for collective bargaining; (2) to interfere with or to question their employees' right to join unions; (3) to interfere with the organization and operation of unions formed by their employees; and (4) to require that an employee join or refrain from joining a labor organization as a condition of employment. In addition to the criminal penalties imposed by the statute, carriers can be enjoined from engaging in activities in violation of these obligations. Practically no criminal cases

---

[1] The discussion that follows is based upon *The Labor Policy of the Federal Government* by Harold W. Metz (1945), pp. 25–40. Documentation will be found there for all statements that are made in this chapter.

69

have been instituted under this law, and very few injunctions have been sought. Nevertheless, during the twenty years since the enactment of the Railway Labor Act of 1926, there has been a great increase in union membership among workers covered by that act. This act as it actually operates provides machinery merely to protect the workers' right to organize.

National Labor Relations Act. The substantive provisions of the National Labor Relations Act of 1935 as passed by Congress appear to protect only the right of workers to organize. From committee reports on the law and from its preamble, it seems that the objective of Congress was not merely to protect the workers' right to organize, but it was to promote and encourage union organization. The National Labor Relations Act, as administered and applied by the National Labor Relations Board, has the effect of positively stimulating and encouraging the development of unions among workers. The methods of administering and enforcing this act differ from those used in the Railway Labor Act. The NLRB is vested with the power to issue cease and desist orders against employers who violate the law, and it also has the authority to reinstate with back pay employees improperly discharged. Its orders are enforced by appeal to a circuit court of appeals, which can secure compliance with them through its contempt power.

Section 7 of the act is a statement of the workers' basic right to engage in concerted action:[2]

Employees shall have the right to self-organization, to form, join, or assist labor organizations, to bargain collectively through representatives of their own choosing, and to engage in concerted activities, for the purpose of collective bargaining or other mutual aid or protection.

This general statement of policy concerning the right to organize is implemented by the first three paragraphs of sec-

[2] 49 Stat. 449, 452.

tion 8. These provisions make it an unfair labor practice for an employer to do any of the following:

(1) To interfere with, restrain, or coerce employees in the exercise of the rights guaranteed in section 7.

(2) To dominate or interfere with the formation or administration of any labor organization or contribute financial or other support to it. . . .

(3) By discrimination in regard to hire or tenure of employment or any term or condition of employment to encourage or discourage membership in any labor organization. . . .[3]

As interpreted and applied by the Board and the courts, these provisions constitute a prohibition against any employer action that might possibly discourage union membership.

The first paragraph of section 8, which prohibits any action by an employer that might restrain, coerce, or interfere with the right of workers to engage in concerted activities, is broad enough to cover all the remaining paragraphs of this section. The employer is forbidden to do anything that will hinder or interfere with the free right of his employees to organize unions of their own choosing. The use of force and violence against union agents or members is prohibited. An employer cannot employ spies to report on union activities. He cannot use bribery nor may he extend special privileges to employees in order to get them to leave a union. The Board has found that an employer violated the law because he offered a union representative a good position "at a high salary provided he would desert the union."

Not only does the law protect the workers' right to organize, but it also makes it illegal for the employer to do anything that may have the result, directly or indirectly, intentionally or unintentionally, of discouraging or interfering with the organizational activities of employees. For example, under some circumstances the employer must permit union agents to enter upon his property to contact his employees, and he cannot prohibit union solicitation of employees upon his property outside

[3] The same.

of working hours. The Board considers that it is an unfair labor practice for an employer to give a wage increase to his employees if there is any evidence that his purpose is to discourage organizational activities.

As applied by the NLRB and the courts, section 8 (1) actually limits the employer's freedom of speech in his dealings with his employees. The Board considers to be an unfair labor practice any utterance of an employer that might discourage union membership or that might encourage employees to join one union rather than another. The Board believes that the act prohibits an employer from making any comment concerning unions, their desirability, and rights. Even where a union has taken a public stand against the existence of an employer's business, he cannot call this fact to the attention of the workers, though the statement was not accompanied by an overt act of coercion. It has been held illegal for an employer to make a correct statement of the rights of employees under the NLRA. Although some of the interpretations of the Board are strange, it is not surprising that the Board has found it an unfair labor practice for an employer to call a union "cut throat."

The Board has held that the effect of an employer's statements concerning a labor organization is to be determined "by an evaluation of the natural consequences of such statements made not by one equal to another, but by an employer to those dependent upon it for their continued employment and livelihood."

The Supreme Court has upheld the Board in its general attitude toward freedom of speech of employers. The Court has declared that coercion of employees by the employer must be evident either in the actual language used by the employer or in some of the surrounding circumstances. If any other action of the employer indicates his opposition to unions, his utterances, although not of themselves coercive, may constitute a violation of the law. On this basis, the Supreme Court has sustained the Board in holding that an employer violated the law by making the following statement, "The Company recognizes the right of every employee to join any union that he may wish to join, and such membership will not affect his position with the Company." In practically every case that has come before it, the Board has been able to find the existence of coercion by considering the employer's utterances in connection with some of his other actions.

The second paragraph of section 8 of the NLRA prohibits employer interference in the formation and operation of unions. This provision was designed to prohibit the establishment of employer-dominated unions. The employer is barred from giving assistance to any labor organization; he cannot advance it money nor may he draft its constitution. The act obviously forbids employer domination, but the Board considers that even an unsuccessful attempt at domination constitutes an unfair labor practice. It is immaterial if the employees joined the union without regard to the employer's attempted interference, and it is not material that they continually desire to belong to the union despite knowledge of the existence of such interference. The attitude of the Board seems to be that any potentiality of employer interference must be eliminated; it has never considered that its task was merely to prohibit activities that positively interfere with the free choice of the employees.

Section 8 (3) prohibits employers from encouraging or discouraging union membership by discriminating in favor of or against employees who join unions, except where a valid closed-shop contract exists. The problem of the closed shop will be considered later in this chapter. In hiring workers and fixing their terms of employment, the employer cannot discriminate against an employee because he is a union member. The Board will order the reinstatement with back pay of any person discharged because of union membership. If an employer refuses to hire a worker because of his union membership, the

Board will compel the employer to give him a job and to pay his salary from the time of the original refusal to hire. Although this decision of the Board and of the Supreme Court may seem surprising, it should be remembered that if the objective of the act is to directly encourage union membership, this is an effective device to attain that objective.

The exact language of section 8 (3) of the act appears to prohibit only such discrimination as will actually encourage or discourage union membership, but the Board has said that the act "forbids the employer to affect or change an employment relationship because of the employee's union membership or activity." If the Board finds that the employer took action only against a group of union members, it practically always assumes the existence of an intent to discriminate against union members. If at any given time an employer discharges only union leaders, the Board infers that the dismissal was discriminatory. When the only employees discharged were those who were active in the formation of a union, the same presumption is made. Should an employer at any time indicate opposition to a union, the Board generally finds that the subsequent dismissal of a union member was because of his union activity. This presumption is followed even though other good reasons for the discharge existed and were alleged, and even though there was no direct evidence that the employer took the action because of the employee's participation in union activities.

The obligation not to discriminate has been extended by the Board to constitute an absolute duty to protect union employees against discriminatory activities of nonunion workers. Where nonunion employees, without the knowledge or approval of the employer, forcibly evicted union employees from the place of work, the Board has held that the employer was guilty of a discriminatory discharge, because he did not give protection to the union members as against the nonunion employees.

Section 8 (3) and also 8 (1), as applied by the Board, make it very difficult for an employer to discipline union employees who refuse to obey his orders. Thus it is an unfair labor practice to discharge an employee because he refused to take a job formerly held by a union official who had been discharged. Workers cannot be discharged because they refuse to work on Labor Day. The discharge of union officials involves definite risks for an employer. The reinstatement by the NLRB of employees discriminatorily discharged involves readily apparent difficulties so far as their future discipline and efficiency are concerned. If an employer discharges a worker who previously had been reinstated by an order of the Board, it would be difficult for him to prove that the second discharge was for good and sufficient reasons and that no element of discrimination was involved. Consequently, the compulsory reinstatement of discharged employees may have detrimental effects upon productive efficiency. To justify such possible interferences with efficiency, one must assume that the gains resulting from union organization of itself are more important to the community than would be the gains resulting from the maintenance of a high level of productive efficiency.

The prohibition against discrimination contained in section 8 (3) leaves the employer without protection against disruptions in operations arising from interunion warfare. Where the employees in a given plant belong to two different unions, and the members of one of these unions refuse to work as long as members of the other organization continue to be employed (while no valid closed-shop agreement exists), it is nevertheless a violation of the act for the employer to solve the problem by dismissing the persons who belong to either of the contending groups, although this is the only way he can prevent production in his plant from being disrupted by a strike. In such a situation there is nothing the employer can do. He cannot secure an injunction against the strike. If he discharges one group of employees and hires only employees who are members of the other group, he violates the NLRA. But if he does not do that, his business might be damaged by a strike.

A union with a majority in a bargaining unit has the exclusive right to bargain for all employees. A minority union nevertheless can strike and disrupt this right of the majority. Strikes by rival labor organizations for organizational and jurisdictional purposes are of course injurious to the employer and to the public. Nevertheless the workers are thus permitted to transgress the rights of properly recognized unions that have the exclusive right to represent the majority of the employees. But here, the majority union and the employer are in the same position; the law offers no method of protection from such interference and disruption by the rival but minority union that cannot legally be recognized by the employer.

The National Labor Relations Act prohibits only employers from interfering with the right of employees to organize. It does not in any way prohibit one organization of employees from interfering with the rights of employees who belong to other labor organizations or who do not desire to become associated with a labor union. The use of force and violence by one union to compel employees to join it is not even considered by the Board in any of its decisions.

RECOMMENDATIONS

Our present policy does not seek merely to protect the right of workers to join unions. It seeks positively to encourage the formation of labor organizations. The workers' right to organize and to engage in concerted action is universally accepted as in accordance with today's basic principles of democracy. Because many employers previously opposed the workers' right to engage in concerted activities, it was necessary for the government to offer some form of protection to ensure that the workers' right to organize would not be transgressed.

But it does not follow from the fact that unions should be protected by government in the right to organize that it is a positive duty of the government to promote labor organization. Whenever a government undertakes to promote any kind of association or organization of special groups in the body politic, whether representing labor, industry, agriculture, or professional groups, it is going beyond the true function of protecting individual or group rights; and it is also creating political difficulties for itself. For these reasons, we conclude that the government should refrain from all efforts intended to promote unionization. Such a movement should result from the spontaneous desires and activities of the interested parties.

Since it is desirable to protect the right to organize, the protection should extend to interference that comes from any source. It is immaterial who interferes with the right to organize. Labor organizations can effectively interfere with the free right of employees to organize or not to organize. But at present our law does not in any way restrict labor groups from interference with these rights. Such coercion from labor groups might be just as disruptive of production and the majority rights as are the activities of an employer. Consequently interference from any source should be forbidden.

The tenor of the decisions of the NLRB is that an employer action that might in any degree influence the choice of workers as between labor organizations is illegal. It does not matter whether the employer's activities interfered with the free right of employees to organize. Most notable have been the decisions of the Board that for all practical purposes have the result of prohibiting any expression of opinion by an employer, concerning the desirability of joining one union as compared with another, on the advantages of not organizing, or even on the rights of employees under the law. Since the employer has to bargain with the organization that the workers select, he does have a real interest in the choice of representatives the workers make. The present decisions of the Board are logical when viewed as a part of a positive program designed to promote unions. Since it is here contended that the protection of the right to organize should be the only objective of the law, it is imperative that the statute be amended to make it clear that it prohibits only overt acts which do interfere with this right. The law should explicitly declare that employers have the right to inform workers concerning their true legal position under the NLRA and that they should be permitted to express an opinion on the desirability of one form of labor organization as compared with another, provided no threat of compulsion is involved in such an expression of opinion.

If the government provides administrative machinery to protect the workers' right to organize, is it desirable for it to protect the workers when they seek to enforce their right to organize through measures of self-help? When an employer refuses to recognize the workers' right to organize, should they be permitted to strike and picket instead of utilizing the machinery provided to enforce the right peacefully? It should be remembered that if workers are permitted to strike to secure the enforcement of the right to organize and to bargain, a minority group might call a strike or take other concerted action that would interfere with the legal rights of a group representing a majority of the employees. If a minority group strikes to get the employer to recognize it as the true representative of the workers, this organization would be breaking the peace in order to compel the employer to violate the rights granted to the group representing a majority of the employees.

If the government provides machinery for the punishment of employers who transgress the rights of their workers, it would hardly seem to be necessary to permit workers to enforce those rights through their own action, without resorting to the methods provided by law. To permit workers to engage in self-help in such circumstances certainly will not promote peaceful industrial relations. There may be far-reaching results for the economy as a consequence of such disruptions in production. If the national objective is primarily to encourage the development of labor organization, it is reasonable to allow measures of self-help though peaceful remedies exist, because it would be appropriate to provide every opportunity for organization. But the protection of the right to organize is only one objective. Another one is the protection of innocent third parties. Hence it is logical to limit the use of self-help where adequate machinery has been established to protect the right.

The law should be designed to discourage workers from resorting to self-help to enforce the right to organize. They should be required to make use of the adequate peaceful remedies provided by law. This might be done by permitting employers to discharge employees who engage in concerted action instead of using the existing administrative remedy established to compel the employer to recognize the union and bargain with it. Injunctive relief should be available to both employers and to the majority union when a minority group resorts to concerted action in order to get an employer to bargain with it in violation of the law. The majority union and the employer should have the right to recover damages from a minority union that engages in concerted action.

UNION PREFERENCE

It is necessary to consider whether it is desirable to permit employers and employees to include in collective agreements clauses providing for various forms of preference for union members and employer aid to unions. The closed shop, the union shop, preferential hiring, and maintenance of membership are the customary forms of union preference. Almost 7 million workers are employed under these various types of clauses. Under the closed shop, all persons employed must be members of the union before they can be employed. Union-shop contracts require that all persons who are employed must within a definite period become members of the union concerned. Under preferential-hiring contracts, members of the union are given preference when new workers are employed or when a layoff is necessary. A maintenance-of-membership clause requires that all persons who are members of the union when the agreement is made or who subsequently become members of it must continue to maintain their union membership during the life of the agreement.

Because of their recent development, maintenance-of-membership clauses require further consideration. The development of maintenance-of-membership contracts is to a very large extent a result of the decisions of the National War Labor Board. During World War II that agency did not want to take the position of promoting the open shop, and it hardly dared to impose the union or closed shop. Consequently, it compromised on the maintenance of membership. The Board presented two primary reasons for imposing maintenance-of-membership provisions on employers in practically all cases where unions requested them. It argued that strong union leadership encouraged war production and that an unstable union membership contributed to an irresponsible union leadership. Secondly, it contended that, because unions declared they would not strike during the war, the government was under a moral and equitable compulsion to take steps to make certain that the unions did not suffer as a consequence of such a pledge. A majority of the members of the Board felt that when conditions of employment were largely set by the government, the direct advantages of union membership would not be fully apparent to the workers and as a result union membership might decline. To prevent such a reduction in membership, they believed that maintenance-of-membership clauses should be imposed on employers. The validity of the arguments for the imposition of these clauses was limited to a war situation.

The Railway Labor Act makes illegal any form of employer preference for union members or of assistance to a union. On the other hand, the National Labor Relations Act specifically legalizes the various types of union-preference clauses, but it provides that such agreements can be made only with the unions that represent a majority of the employees in the bargaining units and that the labor organizations must not have been assisted by an employer. Since most labor organizations desire to have some form of union-preference clause in collective agreements, and since the National Labor Relations Act encourages labor organization, it indirectly promotes union-preference clauses.

As a means of increasing union security and power, unions have demanded preference provisions in agreements. Such provisions prevent employer discrimination against union members. Of course discrimination is now prohibited by law, and consequently the significance of this argument has been reduced. Labor also desires the closed shop, because increased bargaining power results from the restriction of the labor supply that is involved. If one believes in the general increase in bargaining power irrespective of its consequences, this argument has great validity. Unions also contend that since all employees benefit from their activities, all workers should be made to support them. The same argument for compulsory membership could be advanced by employer groups such as trade associations or chambers of commerce.

It is extremely dubious that it is ever desirable to permit the use of any form of union-preference clause, whether it be the closed shop, the union shop, preferential hiring, or maintenance of membership. Such provisions in an agreement tend to create a labor monopoly. Employment opportunities for persons who have never joined a union or who have been expelled from a labor organization are definitely limited. The ability of an individual to shift his employment both as to the place of work and the nature of the job, when economic or other circumstances dictate such a change, is restricted. Labor organizations, under a closed-shop agreement, are in a position to restrict the number of employees who are available for the performance of given types of work. The existence of any form of union-preference agreement restricts employees in the selection of their own bargaining representatives. Obviously persons seeking employment in an establishment where a closed-shop, union-shop, or preferential-hiring agreement exists are not given an opportunity to select their own bargaining representatives. Such prospective employees are not permitted to work if they are not already members of the preferred union or if they refuse to join the organization where a union-shop agreement exists. Under such circumstances it is purely illusory to say that workers have a free right to organize and to select their own bargaining representatives. Consequently, because various forms of union-preference agreements tend to encourage the development of a labor monopoly and to restrict the employment opportunities of workers, and because they tend to make the free selection of bargaining representatives a mere sham, the federal government should not allow employers to make any form of union-preference agreement with the bargaining representatives of their employees. If employers are forbidden to discriminate against unions, they ought not to be permitted to discriminate in their favor. Since employers are now forbidden to discriminate against the organization of unions, the need for union-preference agreements has largely disappeared. It is up to the union to sell itself to the employees by its efficiency in representing them.

Another important form of union assistance is the use of the checkoff. This consists in the collection of union dues and assessments by the employer. Under a checkoff clause the employer automatically deducts the union charges from the employee's pay. Quite generally the employee is not allowed to decide whether or not he desires to give financial support to his labor organization. If the employer acquiesces in the checkoff, the deductions are made from the employee's pay without his authorization. The checkoff is desired by unions because it shifts the task of dues collection to the employer, and the union is thus ensured a steady source of income for the duration of its collective agreement.

Under the Railway Labor Act the checkoff of union dues is absolutely forbidden. In the case of employees covered by the National Labor Relations Act, the checkoff is legal wherever a closed-shop agreement would be legal. The National War Labor Board generally imposed the checkoff if it required the employer to enter into a maintenance-of-membership or a closed- or union-shop agreement. In support of this policy a majority of the Board during the war contended that the unions' pledge not to strike and the limitation of wage increases made it difficult for unions to maintain their membership.

Some supporters of the checkoff contend that trade union leaders should be relieved of the task of dues collection so that they can devote more of their time to organizational and bargaining activities. It is also argued that the checkoff promotes union stability, and thus increases bargaining power.

In opposition to the checkoff, it is urged that by this device the task of dues collection is shifted to the employer and thus he is made to perform a union function. Obviously the cost of dues collection is then borne by the employer.

The checkoff is not entirely consistent with the idea that workers ought to have the right to select their bargaining representatives. If workers have the right of self-organization, they should have the right at any time to withdraw from an organization that they have joined; and one of the most effective methods of withdrawing support from a group is to terminate financial assistance. If employees have the right of self-organization for the purpose of bargaining in their own interest, it would appear that they should have the right to make their bargaining representatives fully responsible to them. Actually, the checkoff tends to reduce the responsibility of union officials to their members.

If one believes in the right of self-organization, and if it is generally assumed that an employer should not assist or discriminate against trade unions, it is illogical to permit them to check off union dues. Obviously, if the government makes it illegal for employers to enter into any form of union-preference agreement, the checkoff would also be illegal.

SUMMARY

The government should protect workers in their right to organize. Any overt act of an employer or of a labor organization that interferes with the right of employees to organize should be prohibited. But this should not be construed to constitute a limitation on the employer's freedom of speech.

Since machinery exists to protect the right to organize, it is not necessary for workers to strike, boycott, or picket to enforce this right. Employers should have the right to discharge workers who engage in concerted action where machinery exists to protect their right to organize. Where a majority union or an employer is injured by an organizational strike, it should be entitled to monetary damages and injunction relief.

Since employer action interfering with or promoting unions is undesirable, the closed shop and all other forms of union preference should be forbidden.

It is not in accordance with good public policy for the government directly to promote the formation of unions.

CHAPTER VII

STRIKES, PICKETING, AND BOYCOTTS

Workers desire the right to organize primarily to engage in collective bargaining. Their main weapons in the bargaining process are strikes, boycotts, and picketing. Public policy toward these implements of industrial warfare will be considered in this chapter.

STRIKES

Current misconceptions concerning strikes make it necessary to analyze in some detail the nature of the legal basis of the right to strike. The right to strike, implicit in existing federal laws, includes not only the right of employees to quit work as a part of concerted activity, but also the right to return to work if and when they so desire. Under the terms of the National Labor Relations Act, strikes are recognized as a legitimate form of concerted activity; and persons on strike continue to be employees. It should be observed that this act does not directly confer the right to strike. Section 7 by implication grants the right, and section 13 provides that: "Nothing in this act shall be construed so as to interfere with or impede or diminish the right to strike." Similarly, the Railway Labor Act carefully states that nothing in the act is to be construed as restricting the right to strike. It was thus tacitly assumed that the right to strike was already existent and guaranteed. The right to strike has usually been identified with the right to quit work. It is asserted that the Thirteenth Amendment, prohibiting slavery, specifically protects the right to strike.

As we now know it, this right has little relation either to the constitutional prohibition of slavery or the guarantee of the right of an individual to quit his job if he doesn't like it. In the first place, a strike is a form of concerted activity; it is a mass movement of men who stop working in order to attain a certain objective.   Second, the strikers do not think of themselves as having quit their jobs, nor does the law assume that they have quit them.   Implicit in the right to strike is the assumption that workers have a right to return to their jobs when their concerted activity is terminated.   Third, the right to strike, as it has developed, involves a general insistence on the part of workers that they should have an untrammeled right to disrupt industrial production and the supply of essential services to the general public.   In a highly complex economy, such a disruption of course frequently causes grave damage to large segments of the population.   Under such conditions, strikes vitally interfere with the rights of others.

There are now few limitations under federal law on the right to strike.   The antitrust laws were formerly construed as constituting a restriction on the right of workers to strike, but as now interpreted they constitute no barrier to the right of labor to strike or to engage in other forms of concerted activity.   The Supreme Court has held that unions are practically free from the criminal provisions of the Antitrust Act, except where they act in concert with employers.   So long as the union acts in its own self-interest and not in collaboration with nonlabor groups, it can commit no violation of the Antitrust Act, although it be demonstrated that the concerted action was designed to restrict interstate commerce substantially.

It is practically impossible at the present time to enjoin a strike in a federal court, even though it is carried on in violation of the Sherman Act or other laws.   This is a result of the Norris-LaGuardia Act of 1932 as interpreted by the courts. Jurisdictional disputes between two unions concerning which group of workers is to perform certain tasks are legal under federal law.   So also are strikes that have for their purpose the restriction of the use of goods made in another state. Similarly, strikes designed to prevent the introduction of new equipment and strikes to compel the employment of unnecessary workers (except in radio broadcasting) are not illegal.

Even strikes for the purpose of compelling an employer to deal with a union other than the one certified by the National Labor Relations Board are protected by the act.

The National Labor Relations Act does not place any significant limits on the right to strike. Even a strike designed to compel an employer to violate the National Labor Relations Act is protected by the act. Although an employer has recognized and bargained with a union that represents a majority of his employees (as he is required to do by the law), a minority group of workers may still strike to get the employer to recognize and bargain with it though this is a violation of the law. The Norris-LaGuardia Act prohibits both the employer and the majority union from securing an injunction against a strike instituted to compel the employer to violate the National Labor Relations Act. The union representing a majority of the employees has no more protection than has the employer who is complying with the law. Even if a union agrees by a collective agreement not to strike, employees who engage in a work stoppage in violation of the agreement cannot be discharged for such activities.

The use of violence in a strike does not generally remove the strike as a whole from the protection of the National Labor Relations Act. The Board normally assumes that violence is an inevitable part of a strike, and consequently the federal government has no interest in taking steps to minimize it. In some instances specific employees who engage in acts of violence might lose the protection of the act, and as a result they can be discharged by their employer, but the misconduct of such employees does not make the whole strike illegal even though their activities are an integral part of a program of concerted action. A strike does not cease to be protected by the National Labor Relations Act, although it is illegal under the law of the state where it occurs.

The War Labor Disputes Act of 1943 prohibits strikes in plants with war contracts until thirty days' notice has been given; but the Board does not consider that a work stoppage called in violation of this law is illegal or improper. In one case the Board held that employees who strike to compel an employer to grant a wage increase not previously approved by the National War Labor Board can be discharged.

Other limitations on the right to strike are few. In line with laws pertaining to mutiny, the crew of a vessel of American registry which engages in a work stoppage away from its home port is subject to criminal penalties, and hence the participants are not protected by the National Labor Relations Act. The War Labor Disputes Act of 1943, under certain circumstances, makes calling, inciting, or assisting a strike a criminal act during World War II. Where the government has taken over a plant producing war materials, it is a crime for any person to urge or persuade the employees to strike, or to give them assistance after a strike has commenced. The actual participation in the strike itself is not illegal. This act also requires that employees of a war contractor must notify the Secretary of Labor and certain other government officials of any labor dispute likely to lead to a strike. After such notice, neither party can change the terms of employment or cease operations for a period of thirty days. If a strike is called without complying with this act, the employer can sue the union for damages, but according to the NLRB he cannot discharge the workers who engaged in the strike.

Striking workers have been accorded by the National Labor Relations Act all the rights granted to employees who are actually working. A person who goes on strike does not thereby cease to be an employee. Employers are prohibited from interfering with concerted activities of their employees, and strikes constitute a form of concerted activity covered by the Act. The Board has implied that it is impossible for an employer to discharge an employee during the course of a strike. The NLRB has the authority to reinstate with back pay any person discriminated against by an employer in violation of the NLRA. Where the strike was not caused by or prolonged by an unfair labor practice of an employer, strikers do not have to be restored to their positions when the strike terminates if their jobs have already been filled by other workers. But if an unfair labor practice of the employer caused the strike or occurred during it, all of the employees who left work are entitled to reinstatement. The striking employees must be reinstated even though this may involve the discharge of some workers who were employed during the strike. Strikers are still employees, although the strike is in violation of the law of the state in which it occurs, or although the work stoppage was in violation of a collective agreement.

The Supreme Court has held that an employee on strike who commits a criminal act as a part of the labor dispute does not have to be restored to his position after the strike has terminated. But the Board generally considers that felonies are the only significant crimes, and conviction is frequently the sole evidence it will accept to show that the illegal act took place. Misdemeanors and various lesser forms of violence are not sufficient cause to justify the discharge of the workers concerned.

Thus the right to strike is protected almost without regard to the objectives of the workers or the methods used. The right to strike, as we now have it, embraces the right to stop work even in violation of the law in many cases. It can be used to get an employer to break a law. Certainly strikes in violation of the law or strikes to get someone else to violate a law cannot be considered to be in the public interest, unless one believes that the right to strike supersedes and transcends all other interests of society.

Our present policy toward strikes is based on the assumption that an increase in bargaining power is a most desirable objective; and since strikes increase the bargaining power of the workers, this form of concerted action must be protected in every possible way. Work stoppages in violation of collective agreements are protected by federal law, although one of the major objectives of our policy of encouraging concerted action is to bring about collective agreements. But if workers are permitted to strike in violation of such agreements, one of the primary reasons why employers sign these contracts disappears. They sign them because they are anxious to free their establishments from interruptions by labor disputes during the life of the agreement.

The federal law protects the workers' right to engage in jurisdictional disputes. In such controversies the only question involved is what group of workers is to perform certain tasks or what organization will be permitted to represent the workers in a given unit. The dispute is not between the employer and his employees, and the bargaining power of the employees as against their employer is not involved. The only thing that is at stake is the prestige and power of one union as compared with another. The public has no interest in promoting one union as against another or in helping one group of workers rather than another to secure jurisdiction over certain tasks.

Sympathetic strikes are fully protected by federal law. This is justified on the assumption that the public interest is advanced by assisting workers who are engaged in a controversy with employers, regardless of the objectives and the methods used. It should be borne in mind, however, that the sympathetic strikers have no direct grievance of their own and have nothing to gain directly from a successful strike. It is purely a weapon designed to strengthen the position of other workers in their controversy. Meanwhile it may have serious repercussions upon economic activity and public welfare.

Even strikes to prevent the introduction of labor-saving devices, or to require the employment of unnecessary workmen, or to prevent the utilization of materials produced outside of the state or city are fully protected by federal law. Certain of such work stoppages do not further the broad goals generally desired by the nation. They hinder the attainment of a higher standard of living, and they are barriers to the reduction of the human effort required in production.

Recommendations. There are several steps that can be taken to discourage and penalize the various kinds of undesirable work stoppages. The activities of labor organizations ought to be brought under the antitrust laws. More specifically, the law should prohibit the co-ordinated, concurrent use of strikes and other forms of concerted action against two or more employers for the purpose of restricting or limiting the movement of goods in interstate commerce. Such a law would be a most important step in breaking down industry-wide bargaining, the shortcomings of which have been discussed in Chapter V. It would make it illegal for a union to strike against two or more employers at the same time, to compel them to grant similar terms of employment. An international union could not tie up a whole industry.

Employees striking in violation of an agreement, or for the purpose of compelling an employer to violate the law, or to accomplish any illegal objective should not be protected by the National Labor Relations Act. The employer should be permitted to discharge such employees. The same thing should apply to sympathetic strikers, those who engage in violence, and those who strike to prevent the utilization of efficient devices and methods. Unions that direct or permit their employees to engage in such work stoppages should be penalized by denying them, for a specified time, the right to represent the employees in the bargaining unit in which the dispute occurred. In all of these cases the union should be liable to compensate the employer for any damages that might result.

PICKETING

Picketing consists of the public display of information concerning the existence of or the issues involved in a labor dispute. The intent of the pickets is to prevent or discourage employees, suppliers, or customers from dealing with the employers involved. Picketing is an important element in industrial warfare since almost all organized workers refuse to cross a picket line because of fear or custom.

Today few limitations are imposed on the right to picket because the Supreme Court has declared that there is an absolute constitutional right to engage in picketing. The decisions of the Court on this question expressly declare that the right to picket is a part of the freedom of speech guaranteed by the First and Fourteenth Amendments. The Court therefore concluded that the right cannot be impaired either by the federal government or by the states. Mr. Justice Murphy speaking for the Court observed in a case involving the freedom to picket:

Freedom of discussion, if it would fulfill its historic function in this nation, must embrace all issues about which information is needed or appropriate to enable the members of society to cope with the exigencies of their period. In the circumstances of our times the dissemination of information concerning the facts of a labor dispute must be regarded as within that area of free discussion that is guaranteed by the Constitution.

The Court's insistence on viewing picketing solely as an exercise of freedom of speech logically leads to this result. The Court completely neglected to consider picketing as an economic weapon designed to cut off the employer from all employees, suppliers, and customers. The only limitations imposed by the Court are that the picketing must occur at the place of business involved, and that it must not be of such a nature as inevitably to cause violence.

Before the Supreme Court clearly declared that the Constitution conferred the right to picket, the federal courts were effectively barred from enjoining picketing by the Norris-La-Guardia Act passed in 1932. Although no labor dispute exists between an employer and his own employees, picketing of his establishment by persons who do not work for him cannot be enjoined. Because of this law, it is also impossible to enjoin picketing that is carried on contrary to the objectives of the National Labor Relations Act. Where an employer properly recognizes and bargains with a union that represents a majority of the employees in an appropriate bargaining unit, another labor organization can nevertheless picket his place of business, even though none of its members are employed in the bargaining unit. It would be an unfair labor practice for the employer to bargain with the picketing union, but the courts hold that such picketing cannot be enjoined. Thus the employer's business may be seriously disrupted because he is obeying the law. Despite the fact that the employees in an establishment have signified to their employer that they do not care to join a specific union, that labor organization may nevertheless picket the place of business of the employer. It would of course be a violation of the National Labor Relations Act for the employer to deal with the picketing union. Even where the objective of a union without any members in a bargaining unit is to secure a closed-shop agreement, the employer cannot enjoin picketing by such a union. Here again it would be illegal for the employer to yield to the demands of the union.

With this constitutional basis of the right to picket, can Congress impose restrictions on picketing in undesirable situations? These decisions of the Supreme Court arose from attempts to suppress picketing by criminal prosecutions and injunctions. They do not involve the question of the obligation to pay damages that might result from engaging in such activities, nor do they involve the right of employers to discharge employees who picket to attain undesirable objectives. At present such a discharge would be a violation of the NLRA, because it would be a discrimination for participation in con-

certed activities.   Merely granting to employers the right to
discharge pickets would be an inadequate method of preventing
improper picketing, for frequently the pickets do not work for
the employer they are picketing. It would be desirable to terminate the bargaining rights of a union which permits its members
(or employees) to picket in violation of the National Labor
Relations Act or for the purpose of causing an employer to
violate a law. A similar penalty should be imposed on unions
that permit pickets to make untrue statements on their banners
or placards, or that permit their members to engage in mass
picketing, or in picketing involving violence. Although the decisions of the Supreme Court would indicate that the courts cannot enjoin picketing, it would be desirable to amend the Norris-
LaGuardia Act so as to permit injunctions to restrict picketing
of the type discussed on page 93.   Such action by Congress
would again put up to the courts the constitutional question
whether or not they will enjoin picketing that is designed for
an illegal or an undesirable purpose, or that contains untrue
statements, or that is carried on by such large numbers of persons as to amount to duress.

BOYCOTTS

A boycott is essentially a combination to get customers to
abstain from dealing with an employer, because of some alleged
grievance against him.   It has been defined by the Supreme
Court as "a combination not merely to refrain from dealing
with the complainant" (an employer) "or to advise or by peaceful means to persuade customers to refrain from dealing," but
also for the purpose of exercising coercive pressure upon such
customers, actual or prospective, in order to cause them to
withhold or withdraw patronage through fear of loss or damage to themselves if they should deal with that employer.

A boycott may consist of a direct campaign to get customers
to abstain from dealing with a given employer, or it may consist
of a refusal by employees to work on goods that have been

previously manufactured, processed, or handled by an employer with whom some labor group had a dispute. The Supreme Court formerly held that boycotts were illegal where their objectives were to reduce interstate commerce in an unreasonable manner. It had declared that it was illegal for workers of one employer to refuse to handle or process goods produced by another employer if such a refusal constituted an unreasonable burden on interstate commerce.

At the present time the Supreme Court apparently will not consider any boycott to be illegal under federal law. The Norris-LaGuardia Act clearly was designed to make it impossible in the future for courts to enjoin boycotts. Under the National Labor Relations Act it is illegal to discharge an employee because he indulges in any form of boycott—which is a form of concerted action protected by the law. In fact, that statute does not permit an employer to protect himself against boycotts designed to compel another producer to violate that act.

Evidence has recently been presented to Congress that clearly demonstrates the anomalous condition of the law relative to boycotts. The NLRB certified that a CIO union represented a majority of the employees in a plant manufacturing neon signs. As a result of this decision, and in full compliance with the law, the employer signed a contract with that union. The electric signs when sold were installed by local electricians, most of whom were members of the AFL International Brotherhood of Electrical Workers. Since the signs were made by workers who belonged to the CIO, the AFL considered that they were made by nonunion labor. Consequently the Brotherhood of Electrical Workers refused to install them, although they were bought by persons who had nothing to do with the original dispute concerning the right to represent the manufacturer's employees. No remedy exists for such a boycott instituted against the producer because he obeyed the National Labor Relations Act.

A boycott which consists of a refusal of workers to handle goods because of labor conditions that existed in the establishments of previous processors clearly extends a labor dispute to persons who are not parties to the original controversy. There is no dispute between the persons engaging in the boycott and the party against whom the boycott is instituted. The improvement of the participating employees' own terms of employment is not involved.

The boycott is purely a form of sympathetic labor activity. It involves the application of pressure indirectly upon a previous producer or processor without regard to the merits of the original dispute. One can logically support our present policy toward the boycott only on the premise that the workers participating in the original dispute are always right and therefore deserve such additional support. The use of this form of concerted action involves a definite potentiality of injury to innocent third parties, who are not in any way connected with the original labor dispute, and who cannot themselves do anything to improve the position of the workers concerned. It imposes unnecessary burdens upon the free flow of goods in interstate commerce, and it maximizes the area and consequences of a labor dispute.

The boycott is an unjustified weapon of industrial warfare and ought to be prohibited by criminal means, injunctions, civil damages, and the suspension of the bargaining rights of unions which utilize the device. An employer ought to be permitted to discharge employees who engage in such activities.

RECOMMENDATIONS

Where the objectives and methods are in accord with the law, the strike is a legitimate form of concerted action. For example, in a dispute concerning the future terms of employment, the strike is a permissible instrument of industrial warfare provided no contract is being violated.

If the objective of a work stoppage is to force an employer to break the law, the strike is improper. Similarly, when workers strike in violation of a contract the stoppage should not be protected. Sympathetic strikes, jurisdictional strikes, and stoppages for the purpose of compelling the employment of unnecessary workers and the use of inefficient processes and machines are against the public interest. The use of force, violence, and intimidation in strikes is contrary to public policy.

Employers should be permitted to discharge workers who take part in such stoppages. Unions that permit these activities should be liable for damages. Injunctive relief against such stoppages should be granted. The bargaining rights of the unions concerned should be suspended.

Since the boycott is designed to injure innocent third parties, it is an inappropriate weapon, and its use should be forbidden.

Picketing should be permitted in all disputes where the objectives sought and the methods used are legal.

CHAPTER VIII

COLLECTIVE BARGAINING

In the two preceding chapters, we have shown how our federal laws protect the rights of the workers to organize and the methods of concerted action used by workers to enforce their rights. Union organization, however, is not an end in itself. The objective of the labor organization is to secure recognition by the employer as the bargaining agent of his employees. The substitution of collective for individual bargaining is a primary objective of our federal labor laws. The collective bargaining process, as well as the bargaining agreement, are the subject matter of this chapter.

COLLECTIVE BARGAINING UNDER THE WAGNER ACT

Section 7 of the Wagner Act confers on employees the right "to bargain collectively through representatives of their own choosing." The law imposes on the employer a positive obligation to bargain collectively. Section 8 states. "It shall be an unfair labor practice for an employer . . . to refuse to bargain collectively with the representatives of his employees, subject to the provisions of Section 9 (a)." The bargaining must be conducted with "representatives designated or selected . . . by the majority of the employees in a unit appropriate for such purposes." The effectiveness of these provisions of the law is shown by the fact that in 1945 more than 14 million workers were covered by collective bargaining agreements. According to the Department of Labor, this number represents about 50 per cent of all employees engaged in industries which have been organized or in industries which unions are making an effort to organize.

Although the Wagner Act imposes a direct obligation on employers to bargain collectively in good faith, it does not set forth any standards to guide the NLRB in determining whether or not an employer has carried out this obligation. The Board is called upon to decide this question when the workers' representative enters a complaint against the employer. The Board has found it difficult to define collective bargaining in explicit terms, or to set up in advance a set of rules or body of principles for deciding cases that vary so greatly. Each case must be decided on its merits.

HOW THE NATIONAL LABOR RELATIONS BOARD INTERPRETS THE LAW

It is now possible, however, after ten years of experience, to state what the reasoning of the Board has been in such matters. The rulings in many specific cases reveal its conception of collective bargaining and its interpretation of the act in respect to the obligation of the employer. The following rulings, derived from many individual cases, have been made by the Board:

1. The employer cannot refuse to meet in person the workers' representative. Bargaining implies a face-to-face discussion of the workers' demands. Bargaining cannot be conducted by correspondence.

2. The employer cannot refuse to recognize as the workers' representative a person or persons not employed by the employer. This of course is consistent with the purposes of the law, since to rule otherwise would be a denial of the right of workers to choose their own representative. In effect it means the employer must deal with the union official designated by the workers involved in the dispute.

3. The employer is prohibited from demanding that the terms of an agreement shall apply only to members of the majority; the agreement must apply to all the workers in the plant, including the employees who are not members of the union. It naturally follows that the employer cannot bargain with individual workers when a majority representative has been chosen. Nor can the employer insist on incorporating in

the agreement his right to listen to and settle individual grievances. Such grievances must be handled by the recognized
representative of the workers. This is an application of the
majority rule. It is an unfair labor practice for an employer
to adjust an individual grievance except through the representative of the majority union.

4. The employer is not bargaining in good faith if he merely
gives a blanket negative reply to the worker's demands; he is
required to give his reasons for his rejection of the specific
demands. The Board has said: "Interchange of ideas, com-
munication of facts peculiarly within the knowledge of either
party, personal persuasion and the opportunity to modify demands in accordance with the total situation thus revealed at
the conference is the essence of the bargaining process."

How far shall the union be permitted to go in securing information to be used in bargaining? In the automobile dispute last spring, the union insisted that the automobile companies open their books so as to determine the basis for their
wage demands. Should this right be accorded to the union as
a part of the bargaining process?

5. The employer is expected to make counterproposals.
This was an issue in the famous Montgomery Ward Case.
Moreover, the counter proposals must not be merely for the
purpose of preventing an agreement from being reached.
Obviously passing on this question involves a personal judgment on the part of the Board. The employer may be offering
terms in good faith, but the Board may regard the proposals
as unreasonable.

6. The employer's refusal to accept a closed shop may not
be advanced as an argument against the proposed agreement.
The Wagner Act, section 8 (3), permits an employer to enter
into a closed-shop arrangement but does not make it obligatory.
This ruling of the Board under the Wagner Act runs directly
counter to an expressed provision in the Railway Labor Act

which prohibits the closed shop. The act contains no language that bears directly on this issue.

7. The employer cannot reject terms of an agreement on the ground that his competitors do not operate under terms of the proposed agreement.

8. The employer is obligated to continue negotiations until an impasse has been reached. The burden of proof generally rests with the employer. He must demonstrate to the satisfaction of the Board that further negotiations are futile. This is often difficult to do, and the Board must decide the issue.

9. Although the law does not compel either party to come to an agreement, the employer cannot refuse to sign a written agreement once the terms have been agreed upon.

10. In assessing the employer's obligations, the Board distinguishes between a renewal of contract and the negotiation of the original agreement. In the case of a renewal, the Board has held that the employer has acted in good faith if he merely offers to renew the terms of the existing agreement. In the negotiation of an original agreement, the Board extended its authority to pass on the substantive terms of the agreement.

It is clearly apparent that in carrying out the collective bargaining provisions of the Wagner Act, the Board not only establishes the procedure to be observed, but has also to a certain degree set itself up as an arbiter in passing on the substance of an agreement. The Board has used its wide discretionary power to pass on the question as to whether or not the terms demanded by the union or the counterproposals offered by the employer best carry out the purposes of the act. This function was never intended by the authors or the proponents of the bill. In reporting the bill to the Senate, the Senate Committee on Education and Labor stated:

The committee wishes to dispel any possible false impression that this bill is designed to compel the making of agreements or to permit governmental supervision of their terms. It must be stressed that the duty to bargain collectively does not carry with it the duty to reach an agreement, because the essence of collective bargaining is that either party shall be free to decide whether proposals made to it are satisfactory.[1]

Despite this declaration by the Senate Committee, the fact remains that the act did impose on the NLRB the duty of administering the law, including the provision which imposes on the employer a positive obligation to bargain collectively in good faith. Congress was at fault in its failure to define clearly the power of the Board in the interpretation of this provision of the act. It certainly was never the intention of Congress to have the Board function as a conciliator or arbitrator. When the bill was being considered in Congress, an effort was made by the Secretary of Labor to put the NLRB within the Department of Labor. One reason for not doing so was the fear that the Board might get involved in the conciliation service which the Department was performing.

Since the NLRB has wide discretionary power in matters relating to collective bargaining procedures as well as to the substantive terms of the agreement, it is exceedingly important that the Board members be judicially minded. Unfortunately, some of the Board members have lacked this impartiality; this was especially true in the early years of the administration of the act. In cases where the workers entered a complaint against the employer for failing to bargain collectively, the Board frequently adjudged the employer guilty on unsubstantial evidence. The antiunion record of employers in the years before the Wagner Act was passed was used against the employer in deciding cases. It must be admitted that many employers reluctantly accepted the Wagner Act, until after it was declared constitutional by the Supreme Court in 1937. Many of the large companies in steel, rubber, and automobiles resisted collective bargaining, for several years after the Wagner Act was passed. This combination of circumstances—the bias

[1] *National Labor Relations Board,* S. Rept. 573, 74 Cong. 1 sess., p. 12.

of the Board members and the unco-operative spirit of many larger employers—accounts for some of the prejudiced decisions of the Board. The rulings of the Board should now be re-examined in the light of the changed situation. Unions are no longer weak in bargaining power; and the Wagner Act has been generally accepted by industry.

LABOR NOT OBLIGATED TO BARGAIN COLLECTIVELY

The Wagner Act imposes no obligation on labor to bargain collectively. This omission is understandable in view of the relatively weak position of labor at the time the act was passed. Conditions have changed radically since 1935. Many unions now enjoy a monopoly control of labor in the industries in which they operate. A union that wishes to punish an employer can refuse to bargain with him, and thus refuse to accord his employees union status. This may be damaging, if not destructive, to an employer's business in an industry in which a closed shop prevails.

To show that this is not an academic question, we cite the case of the Hunt Motor Transportation Company of Philadelphia. The employees of this firm affiliated with the AFL and demanded a closed shop. The employer refused and a strike followed. Bitter feeling developed, and the union decided not to do business with the Hunt Company. To punish the company, however, the union persuaded the Atlantic and Pacific Company to withdraw its business from Hunt on the ground that the closed-shop agreement with the Atlantic and Pacific debarred it from using the services of the Hunt Company. The employer expressed a desire to come to terms with the union, but the union refused to bargain with Hunt. The latter sought a new client, and again the union stepped in and ordered the new client to refrain from doing business with the Hunt Company. The Wagner Act afforded the employer no remedy. There may not be many cases of this kind, but the Hunt case illustrates the inequity and unfairness in the labor act, in failing to impose on labor the obligation to bargain collectively.[2]

The one-sided character of the provisions for collective bargaining is illustrated in the case of the demands of John L. Lewis in the spring of 1946. He called upon the mine owners to bargain collectively but refused to state his wage demands. He insisted that before he reveal his wage demands the mine owners must agree to create a welfare fund, to be administered exclusively by the United Mine Workers Union. By this procedure he brought about an impasse, culminating in a strike. He thereby forced the government to intervene and take over the mines. Then the government came to terms with Lewis; he was granted not only a welfare fund but also a substantial wage increase. The mine owners have had no voice in fixing the wage structure now imposed on their industry. There was no opportunity for collective bargaining between the union and the mine owners because of the refusal of Lewis to bargain collectively in good faith with the mine owners. He was acting within his rights; the law is deficient in not imposing this obligation on unions that claim and receive all the privileges accorded labor under the Wagner Labor Act.

The exercise of monopoly power of labor in a single industry so essential as coal illustrates how the collective bargaining provision of the Wagner Act is nullified. What has happened in the coal industry might occur in any one of many essential industries. What if a combination of powerful unions simultaneously took the position that Lewis took in this coal crisis? Suppose they flatly demand a certain wage increase, "or else," as Lewis has continually done. Under such conditions our

[2] The Hunt Company brought action for damages against the union under the Sherman Antitrust Act. The Supreme Court ruled that the refusal of employees to work for the Hunt Company did not constitute a violation of the Antitrust Act in this case. The Court ruled that "It was not a violation of the Sherman Act for laborers in combination to refuse to work. They may sell or not sell their labor as they please, and upon such terms and conditions as they choose, without infringing the antitrust laws." *Hunt et al.* v. *Crumboch*, 325 U.S. 821 (1945).

nation might be faced with a multiple industry shut-down, without any opportunity for free collective bargaining as was intended by the Wagner Act.

THE SCOPE OF BARGAINING AGREEMENTS

Unions have been attempting to widen the scope of collective agreements. The tendency has been to encroach more and more on the long-recognized prerogatives of management. For example, the unions have demanded that the NLRB permit foremen, if they so desire, to organize and affiliate with national unions, which embrace all the workers in industry. The NLRB has vacillated on this issue. The Board has taken jurisdiction and decided that foremen can organize unions of their own and also affiliate with national bodies. It remains for the Supreme Court to rule on this controversial matter. The Wagner Act defines an employer as "any person acting in the interest of an employer, directly or indirectly." Supervisors, including foremen, have always been regarded as acting in this capacity. To rule otherwise is to place the foreman in the impossible position of serving two masters—his employer and the national union of which he might be a member. How embarrassing this might become was illustrated in a case in which a foreman was found guilty of violating the Wagner Act in influencing a worker in his attitude toward one particular union as against another. The employer sought to discipline the foreman but was denied this right under the same law.

If the workers want to bargain concerning the plants to be shut down, the employer must bargain. Where the employees desire to bargain relative to the plants where given parts of an assembled product are to be made, the employer must bargain about it. The employer is obligated to bargain with his employees concerning "rates of pay, wages, hours of employment or other conditions of employment." What does "other conditions of employment" mean? The law does not define the other conditions of employment which are the subject of bargaining, nor does it state the prerogatives of management that are beyond the scope of the bargaining process.

There is in the offing a demand on the part of some unions that the employers agree to a guaranteed wage. If the employers should refuse to agree to this proposal, would the Board have the right to say that the employer is not bargaining in good faith and therefore adjudged guilty under the law? In the light of this trend it seems that Congress ought to lay down a policy of guidance for the NLRB as to the scope of collective agreements.

COLLECTIVE BARGAINING UNDER THE RAILWAY LABOR ACT

Our discussion of collective bargaining to this point has been confined to the Wagner Labor Act, which is not applicable to transportation. Under the Railway Labor Act as amended in 1934, the obligation to bargain collectively is imposed on the carriers and their employees in these words: "It shall be the duty of all carriers, their officers, agents, and employees to exert every reasonable effort to make and maintain agreements concerning rates of pay, rules, and working conditions." [3] Bargaining by the carriers must be with the representative of the employees in the bargaining unit which has been designated by the National Mediation Board. The employees can enforce this latter provision by an injunction restraining the carrier from dealing with any other group.

The Railway Labor Act does not compel an agreement, but it does command that definite preliminary steps be taken by both parties in an effort to reach an agreement. In contrast with the provisions of the Wagner Act, this law merely prescribes the procedures by which a collective agreement might be reached. Perhaps this was sufficient in the railroad industry because railroad unions had a long experience in dealing with the carriers. Over a long period, both management and the railroad brotherhoods had been educated to the use of such

---

[3] 48 Stat. 1185, 1187.

procedures for establishing a satisfactory labor arrangement. Therefore collective bargaining has spread with little friction to parts of the industry where agreements had not yet been effected at the time the Railway Labor Act was passed.

The Railway Labor Act also provides machinery for facilitating and effecting a bargaining agreement. This is done through the National Mediation Board or special emergency boards. The act also created a National Railroad Adjustment Board for the purpose of settling disputes that arise from the interpretation of existing agreements.

DIFFICULTIES IN THE ENFORCEMENT OF LABOR AGREEMENTS

The unions as well as the employers expected industrial peace to flow from the agreements arrived at through collective bargaining. Both parties overlooked one important aspect— enforceability. When the Wagner Act was passed, it was generally assumed that the labor agreements were enforceable on both parties like ordinary contracts. When violations occurred, it was discovered that it was both difficult and cumbersome to apply the law of contracts to a labor agreement.

Unions are creatures of the states and operate under state laws; action for damages against them must be brought in state courts; they cannot be reached under federal law. Since unions for the most part are unincorporated, they cannot be sued except in a few instances where the state law expressly provides for this. Action for damages, when brought into state courts, is decided on the basis of the common law. There is no uniformity among the 48 states in the application of these common-law principles. Moreover, legal authorities seriously question the applicability of the principle of common law to the present-day collective bargaining agreement.

Since unions are generally regarded as partnerships or membership associations without a legal personality separate from that of their members, it is frequently difficult for the employer to sue the union without serving legal process on each of its members. Obviously this is not easy, but without the service of such process, in many states it would be impossible to attach the union funds. The courts of many states have found it impossible to devise a legal theory that justifies a suit against the union as the agent and representative of its members. Some states have been able to surmount this problem, but others have not seen a way out.

The Norris-LaGuardia Act also limits the responsibility of union members for acts of the officials of the union. Only where the specific activities of the officers or agents have been previously or subsequently authorized by members, are the members, themselves, personally responsible for such acts.

If a union feels that an employer has violated an agreement, the federal law permits the union to determine whether it will sue the employer for damages or whether it will strike to secure its interpretation of the agreement. Moreover, if the alleged violation of the agreement by the employer also constitutes an unfair labor practice, the union can get the NLRB to prosecute the employer for such activities. While the union has a right to use the strike as a weapon to enforce its interpretation of an agreement, the employer under comparable circumstances is not permitted to use the lockout against his employees.

The collective bargaining agreement is a most useful instrument, providing the terms of the agreement can be enforced with equal justice to both parties. Unfortunately, Congress has neglected this important aspect of the industrial labor relations problem. Since the Wagner Act imposes an obligation on the employer to bargain collectively, Congress ought to provide the necessary legal machinery for the fair and just enforcement of the terms of the agreement arrived at through collective bargaining. Some method must be devised for protecting the employer against any damage suffered by virtue of unions violating the terms of an agreement. So long as unions are not faced with this responsibility, a repetition of strikes led by irresponsible labor leaders may be expected.

RECOMMENDATIONS

To preserve and strengthen collective bargaining the following steps should be taken:

1. The obligation to bargain collectively should be imposed on employees as well as employers.

2. The nature of the obligation to bargain collectively should be clearly defined.

3. The subject matter to be covered by collective agreements should be delineated by law.

4. The obligation imposed by collective agreements should be enforceable against both parties through the use of appropriate judicial machinery.

5. The law should specifically provide that unincorporated unions are suable for violation of the terms of a labor agreement.

CHAPTER IX

THE GOVERNMENT AND THE BARGAINING UNIT

The government requires employers to bargain collectively with the representative of a majority of their employees, and as a result it has become involved in determining the units into which workers are to be organized for such bargaining purposes. If employers are to know with which groups of their employees they must bargain, it is desirable for someone to designate the appropriate bargaining units. Consequently, the government has created machinery to determine the composition of the units that are appropriate for bargaining purposes, and also to determine who represents a majority of the workers within such units. Congress imposed the task of settling these questions on the National Labor Relations Board and the National Mediation Board, each acting in its respective field. Because of the extensive coverage of the National Labor Relations Board, and because that agency is presented with the more difficult problems, the ensuing discussion of the selection of the bargaining unit will be concentrated on the work of this establishment in the performance of this task.

Any type of government activity for the purpose of designating bargaining units is incompatible with one of the cherished ideas of the American labor movement. A basic assumption of organized labor in this country has been that the labor movement is purely voluntary in nature. Organized labor has long insisted that the formation and structure of unions should be determined by labor alone, completely free from any governmental control. For almost fifty years the American Federation of Labor considered itself to be the sole center and source of the legitimate labor movement in the United States (outside of the railroad brotherhoods). Charters granted by the AFL demarcated the areas within which each of the so-called inter-

110

national unions could organize workers. The charter conferred an exclusive right to organize. No other group affiliated with the AFL supposedly could organize the workers covered by the charter of another. The choice of which union a worker of a given skill could join generally was not his. The AFL made that decision for him. But where there is any dispute concerning which union is to represent the workers the decision is now in the hands of the government. By assuming the role of demarcating the boundaries of bargaining units, the government largely determines the labor organization that will represent the workers in a given bargaining unit.

SIGNIFICANCE OF THE BARGAINING UNIT

The designation of the appropriate bargaining unit by the National Labor Relations Board has important implications for both the employees and the public. The grant of exclusive bargaining rights to the majority of employees in a unit makes the selection of the unit of great import to the workers. One of the fundamental principles that has been adopted concerning collective bargaining is that the representatives chosen by a majority of the workers in a unit have the exclusive right to bargain for all of the workers in that unit. The Senate Committee on Education and Labor in reporting the National Labor Relations Act to the Senate in 1935 justified the majority principle in the following terms:

The object of collective bargaining is the making of agreements that will stabilize business conditions and fix fair standards of working conditions. Since it is well-nigh universally recognized that it is practically impossible to apply two or more sets of agreements to one unit of workers at the same time, or to apply the terms of one agreement to only a portion of the workers in a single unit, the making of agreements is impracticable in the absence of majority rule. And by long experience, majority rule has been discovered best for employers as well as employees. Workers have found it impossible to approach their employers in a friendly spirit if they remained divided among themselves. Employers likewise, where majority rule has been given a trial of reasonable duration, have found it more conducive to harmonious labor relations to negotiate with representatives chosen by the majority than with numerous warring factions.[1]

Any alternative scheme of proportional or minority representation would probably have undesirable results for both workers and employers. Proportional or minority representation means instability of bargaining groups. It constitutes an open invitation for continuous fractionalization among the workers involved. It therefore complicates the bargaining task for the employer.

The establishment of the majority-rule principle, it should be recognized, means that minority groups of workers in any bargaining unit will have no voice in the selection of representatives or in the bargaining process. Consequently, workers with special skills and interests now have a direct voice in collective bargaining only if they constitute a majority in a separate unit. Where exclusive bargaining rights are granted to the majority, an agency is bound to be criticized when it designates bargaining units—in effect election districts—because it inevitably influences the choice of representatives.

It should be emphasized that the Board designates only the bargaining units. It does not itself designate the bargaining representatives; it does not outrightly select this union or that union to represent the employees. The workers in the bargaining unit established by the Board choose the bargaining representatives themselves. But the composition of the bargaining unit frequently is decisive in determining which of several possible bargaining representatives will be designated by a majority of the workers. Consequently, the unit selected by the Board is often a most significant factor in determining which union will represent a given group of employees.

[1] National Labor Relations Board, S. Rept. 573, 74 Cong. 1 sess., pp. 13–14.

THE NATIONAL LABOR RELATIONS BOARD AND THE BARGAINING UNIT

Section 9 (b) of the National Labor Relations Act gives to the National Labor Relations Board the power to "decide in each case whether, in order to insure to employees the full benefit of their right to self-organization and to collective bargaining, and otherwise to effectuate the policies of this Act, the unit appropriate for the purpose of collective bargaining shall be the employer unit, craft unit, plant unit, or subdivision thereof." The law imposes on the Board the task of determining the unit. It alone must make this decision. If the Board desires, it can permit the employees to express their choice by ballot as to what unit they prefer. The results of such a ballot constitute only advice to the Board. That agency is not bound to abide by the preference of the employees, although it generally follows their wishes as thus expressed. But the Board does not have to use the ballot in any given case, and it frequently does not attempt to discover the wishes of the workers.

To guide the Board in selecting the appropriate unit, no clear standards are contained in the law. It should be noted specifically that such a determination by the Board is supposed "to insure to employees the full benefit of the right of self-organization and to collective bargaining, and otherwise to effectuate the policies of this Act." One of the major "policies of this Act" is to equalize bargaining power (section 1) and to equalize bargaining power meant to the proponents of the law to increase the bargaining power of the workers. Thus in performing the task of selecting the appropriate bargaining unit, one of the objectives of the Board under the NLRA is to determine the desire of the employees, and another objective is to increase the bargaining power of the workers. In some cases the independent application of these two standards might lead to quite different results.

In making a choice among the possible types of units mentioned in the act, the Board has used the two standards in diverse ways in different decisions. The Board, itself, refuses to state with any precision the rules that it is likely to apply in determining the unit in any specific case. Because of the varied pattern of industrial organization, it would be difficult to formulate such principles with any degree of precision.

It is where the workers themselves are not agreed on the unit that the Board is confronted with the difficult problem of selecting it. If no dispute exists among the employees, the Board will designate any bargaining unit desired by the workers.

In settling the conflicts between the claims of different groups of employees, various principles have been utilized by the Board. It asserts that as far as possible it has attempted to fit the bargaining unit to the existing bargaining practices. If the workers previously have been organized on a broad basis, extensive units often have been found to be appropriate. But where the employees have not been organized on a broad basis, small units sometimes have been considered suitable. Generally, the Board has attempted to pick as large a unit as is feasible in order to bring the benefits of collective bargaining to the greatest possible number of workers. This obviously is designed to increase the workers' bargaining power. The maximization of bargaining power has been used as a basis for justifying the inclusion in one bargaining unit of employees working in several different plants, and it is also the reason employees of more than one employer are sometimes included in the same unit.

In selecting bargaining units, the Board considers the community of interest of the workers. As a rule, production and maintenance employees in the same plant will be included in the same unit. Where work is passed on from one plant to another and the production in one plant is influenced by the quality of work done in another, both plants are frequently included in the same unit.

The most difficult cases for the Board to decide are those involving conflicting claims of craft and industrial unions. It has attempted to solve some of these disputes by permitting the workers to express their preference. This practice is in accord with the principle of self-determination as embodied in the law. The Board states that when it concludes that the equities are equally balanced between the conflicting claims for a craft unit as against an industrial unit, it will allow craft workers within the larger unit to determine by an election whether they desire to bargain separately from the rest of the workers or whether they prefer to be included as a part of the larger unit. But if the workers of a specific craft are to be permitted to express such a preference for separate bargaining, it must be demonstrated, first, that the work they perform has normally been considered to be a separate craft, and second, that members of that craft must actually be employed at the time of the election. Where a collective agreement already exists covering a wider unit, the Board will not permit a craft unit to be carved out of it, even though a majority of the members of the craft should so desire. But it should be remembered that only when the Board itself finds that the equities are equally divided between a craft and an industrial unit will it give the workers an opportunity to express a choice.

The decisions of the Board do not always make it clear whether several plants belonging to the same employer are to be included in the same unit or whether each plant is to constitute a separate bargaining unit. The Board generally favors a multiple-plant unit, because on this basis the bargaining power of the workers tends to improve. Where a company-wide unit is desired by the employees in all the plants, the Board usually establishes such a unit. This is especially true where a common personnel policy is applied to the different plants, and where the plants are interdependent elements in the productive process.

Often the Board has included in multiple-plant units only those plants in which the union making the request already represents a majority of the employees. If all the plants of an employer were to be included in one unit and the employees in some have not been organized, a majority of the workers in the unit as a whole might reject the union, and then none of the employees would have the benefits of collective bargaining. But there is no uniformity in the decisions of the Board, and consequently it is not possible to determine in advance whether the Board will permit the employees in a given plant to vote on the question of whether they desire a plant or an employer unit.

Although the Board has stated these various principles for determining what constitutes an appropriate bargaining unit, it leaves for itself wide discretion in selecting the unit. These principles overlap and are not formulated with such exactness as to permit one to predict how the Board will apply them in a given case. There is some inconsistency between the only two guides that Congress provided for the Board in selecting the appropriate unit. Congress has declared that one of the objectives of the Board should be to increase the bargaining power of the workers. The application of this principle would tend to favor the development of large bargaining units. The other goal set by Congress is that the Board should guarantee to the workers their right to self-organization. The smaller the unit the greater is the self-determination allowed to separate groups of workers with diverse interests, who might constitute minorities if they were included in a larger unit. The smaller the unit the less, generally speaking, is its bargaining power; so in some cases the protection of the workers' right of self-determination might clash with the goal of increasing bargaining power. Where the two objectives are in conflict, the Board has tended to favor increasing bargaining power, even though in the process of selecting larger units some workers inevitably become minority groups and thereby lose their self-determination.

MULTIPLE-EMPLOYER BARGAINING UNITS

Because the multiple-employer bargaining unit presents problems of special significance to the economy, it deserves separate consideration. Where the employees of several different employers desire to bargain as a single unit, the Board frequently will designate a multiple-employer unit if there has been collective bargaining on that basis. In some cases such units embrace only the employees of a few employers; in others they include practically all of the workers in a whole industry.

Under the National Labor Relations Act the Board has only limited opportunities to establish or assist in maintaining multiple-employer units. Before the Board can designate such a unit, there must already exist an association of employers with authority to bargain. This requirement is inherent in the definition of the term employer that is contained in the National Labor Relations Act. Section 2 provides: "The term 'employer' includes any person acting in the interest of an employer" and the term person "includes one or more individuals, partnerships, associations, corporations, legal representatives," and the like. The framers of the act purposefully phrased these definitions in this way because they were anxious to ensure that the Board could not impose multiple-employer bargaining where this had not already been practiced before its decision.

The Board has been willing to certify multiple-employer units because this tends to strengthen the bargaining power of the workers. It has also said that it favored such units because it considered desirable the establishment of uniform wages among competing plants. The Board generally requires the continuation of a multiple-employer unit, even though the workers in one establishment in such a unit desire to leave that unit and bargain on a plant or a single-employer basis. Where collective bargaining actually has been in operation on the basis of the multiple-employer unit, the workers of one plant will not be permitted to withdraw and bargain separately. The Board opposes the break-up of such units because it believes that this might lead to a reduction in the bargaining power of the employees. In a case where multiple-employer bargaining had been followed, but employees of one employer requested that they be designated a separate unit, the Board observed:

> We are convinced that the full benefit of their right to self-organization and to collective bargaining cannot be insured to the employees by breaking up the collective bargaining unit which has been established by a long history of contractual relations between the operators and miners of the anthracite region.[2]

Here the Board appears to consider that the maintenance of bargaining power is more important than the protection of the workers' freedom of self-organization.

For the Board to approve of a multiple-employer unit, not only must collective bargaining have been practiced on that basis, but the existing employers' bargaining association must have the authority to bargain for and bind its members. What this authority really means is far from clear. The employers' association probably could not legally bind its members not to operate their plants if the association was unable to secure the desired terms from the union. It would be illegal for the members to agree that the association should penalize an employer who operated his plant when the bargaining association ordered him to cease production as a step in the bargaining process.

Obviously such an agreement would violate the Sherman Antitrust Act, and the conduct of the employers would also be contrary to the National Labor Relations Act. In fact, any agreement between employers not to produce would violate the antitrust laws. It would be a lockout in violation of the NLRA for employers to shut their plants until the union met their terms. Consequently, it seems that the employers' asso-

[2] *Stephens Coal Co.,* 19 NLRB 98, 110 (1940).

ciation probably would never have as great bargaining power as the union representing the workers included in the unit, since it would be unable to force its members to close their plants as a bargaining maneuver. Nor could it penalize a member who signed a collective agreement not in conformity with the principles arrived at by the association.

Other government agencies have done more than the NLRB to promote industry-wide collective bargaining. For example, the National Mediation Board has looked with favor upon the development of industry-wide bargaining for the determination of working conditions on railroads. Thus in one of its annual reports it observed, "the consummation of such nation-wide understandings is . . . deserving of all possible encouragement and commendation." The practice of industry-wide bargaining on railroads was encouraged by the carriers in 1932, when they sought a general wage reduction for all roads at the same time.[8]

Several wartime agencies have done much to promote or to facilitate the practice of collective bargaining on an industry-wide basis. During World War II, the Office of Production Management and the War Production Board stimulated the development of bargaining for shipbuilding on a regional basis to assist in the equalization of wages among the Pacific, Gulf, and Atlantic Coasts. The Maritime Commission and the War Shipping Administration encouraged multiple-employer bargaining in the shipping field. In the construction of airplanes, the War Production Board assisted in the development of industry-wide action, especially among manufacturers of air frames on the Pacific Coast. The National War Labor Board helped to bring about changes in wages and working conditions on an industry-wide basis in steel, rubber, nonferrous metal mining, and lumber. In most of these cases the initiative in

[8] In a few other instances employers initiated industry-wide bargaining; for example, in the full-fashioned hosiery industry, see R. A. Lester and R. A. Robie, *Wages under National and Regional Collective Bargaining* (1946), p. 46.

developing the multiple-employer approach came from the unions, but the Board tended to favor the practice because this made possible wage stabilization throughout a whole industry and because it lightened its work load. Although the Board is no longer in existence, the results of its activities continue to be evident.

There are instances where the Conciliation Service has facilitated unions in carrying out their demands for industry-wide bargaining. This was noticeably true in the negotiations for wage increases in the petroleum refining industry in the autumn of 1945.

RECOMMENDATIONS

With this background of our present policy toward the problem of the bargaining unit, the issues of public policy involved can be considered. The basic goals of our society and the fundamental principles of our labor program must to a large extent determine the standards that are to be used in deciding what constitutes the appropriate bargaining unit.

Our present objective of promoting labor organizations in order to increase the workers' bargaining power has complicated the task of the National Labor Relations Board in the designation of the appropriate bargaining unit. It has already been demonstrated that it is desirable for the federal government to protect the workers' right of self-organization, rather than to promote positively labor organizations. If our policy and law were revised to provide that the government should protect only the workers' right to organize, this would eliminate many of the basic conflicts evidenced in the selection of the bargaining unit by the National Labor Relations Board.

It is desirable that workers be encouraged to develop and acquire greater skills, because this promotes increased output with reduced human effort. Accordingly, it would seem that it would be desirable to permit groups of workers with specialized skills to constitute separate bargaining units. However, the internal organization of unions is such as to lead almost inevitably in the opposite direction. Union officials naturally desire to obtain maximum support among the union members in connection with labor contracts. Hence equal treatment must be given to all workers, skilled and unskilled, which usually means in practice that all are given the same increase. The result is that the incentive to develop or acquire greater skills is reduced.

A major principle of our labor policy should be to minimize the area of labor disputes so as to reduce the possibility of public disturbance and disruption that results from them. The smaller the number of workers and the amount of production involved in any dispute, the less is the likelihood of government intervention and a political settlement.

To facilitate the attainment of such an objective, bargaining units should not embrace employees of more than one employer. This is necessary in order to minimize the possibility of the complete cessation of the entire production of a necessary commodity or service. In an industry-wide unit, equality of bargaining power between the parties can be attained only by suspending the antitrust laws. Only if the employers by concerted action can close down production as the union can, will the bargaining power of the parties really be equalized. The undesirability of such practices by employers is generally taken for granted. Most disputes concerning the conditions of employment where only a single employer is involved can be settled by the use of economic weapons without an extensive disruption of production that normally would impose great burdens upon the consuming public. In most instances, alternative sources of supply are available to the consuming public.

To attain an equitable distribution of the fruits of technological gains is another major reason why bargaining units should not embrace more than one employer. A sizable proportion of the technological gains in any enterprise should be distributed to the consumer as well as to labor and capital. Since such gains are actually realized in specific establishments, their distribution can take place only in the individual companies. If workers are to be encouraged to increase their efficiency, they must receive some of the gains resulting from the application of their own efforts. This means that bargaining should take place on the basis of units that embrace only a single employer, or in some cases single plants.

Proceeding from the foregoing discussion, certain suggestions may be made concerning the designation of the appropriate bargaining unit by the National Labor Relations Board. If employers are to bargain with their employees, it is inevitable that some agency must determine who constitutes the representative of the employees in a unit appropriate for bargaining purposes.

Since it is desirable to localize industrial disputes, no bargaining unit should include the employees of more than one employer. The Board should not be given the authority to designate multiple-employer bargaining units, even though both employers and employees should so desire. A mere prohibition against the designation of multiple-employer units by federal agencies (such as the NLRB) will not of itself end the practice of industry-wide bargaining where it now exists, nor will such a prohibition definitely preclude the spread of this form of bargaining. Other government agencies, such as the Conciliation Service, should not attempt to encourage this practice. The use of concerted action by workers to bring about industry-wide bargaining should be regarded as a violation of the antitrust laws. Obviously though all of these suggestions are followed, industry-wide bargaining might not be completely eliminated.

In selecting the bargaining unit, the main task of the Board must be to determine the wishes of the employees of a given company. The application of the principle of self-determination would mean that if any particular group of workers in a company—either those who are employed in a specific plant or those possessing a special skill—desires to bargain separately from the rest of the employees, the Board must give the employees in that group a chance to show by ballot whether or not a majority desires to bargain separately. The mere existence of a previous practice of bargaining on a company or a plant-wide basis should not preclude the workers from having a chance to express such a choice. That is to say, the law should permit bargaining units to be organized on the basis of crafts, skills, plants, or for all of the employees of a single employer.

As a rule, only employees are permitted to request the Board to certify a bargaining representative. After much criticism the Board has allowed employers to petition for the designation of bargaining representatives when two or more unions claim to represent a majority of the employees in a unit. But if only one union demands bargaining rights, the employer cannot raise the question of whether it represents a majority of his employees. The union can call strikes and engage in other forms of concerted action to coerce an employer into bargaining with it, even though it does not represent a majority of the employees. Where it has not attained a majority status, the employer is not obligated to bargain with it, yet he has no means of protection against its concerted action. One solution of this problem would be to permit the employer to petition the Board to designate a bargaining representative whenever a union is engaged in concerted action to secure recognition. Another method would be to prohibit any union from carrying on concerted action of any type unless it had been designated as a bargaining representative.

CHAPTER X

THE ORGANIZATION OF UNIONS

In this chapter the relation of the government toward the internal organization and operation of unions will be considered. Should the government attempt to determine how unions should be organized and who is to be admitted to membership or who is to be expelled from them? In designating a labor organization as a bargaining representative, should the government seek to determine whether the activities of the organization are in conformity with national labor policy?

The federal government has given certain important rights to unions. It has conferred upon them the right to engage in various forms of concerted action, and this right can be used to disrupt production and distribution. Such disruptions of production can injure persons who are not in any way connected with the dispute and who are powerless to grant the demands of the workers. Because of the normal consequences of concerted activities of unions, the public has some interest in the organization and functioning of these groups.

The grant by the government of exclusive bargaining rights to majority unions justifies some public regulation of the organization and operation of them. We have appropriately adopted the principle that the majority union has the exclusive right to bargain. This means that in any bargaining unit the union which represents a majority of the employees has the exclusive right to bargain collectively for all of the employees. Such an organization alone has the exclusive right to speak collectively for all of the employees. If the majority union has the exclusive right to bargain for all employees, it is only fair that all employees should have the right to become and remain members of the union and to participate in its deliberations on an equal footing. Consequently, the grant of exclusive bargaining rights justifies federal regulation of the membership of labor organizations.

At the present time, the federal government does not exercise any control over the formation and membership of labor organizations. Unions are strictly the creatures of state law. They are generally associations and (rarely) corporations established under the laws of the several states. The national government merely assumes the existence of unions; it does nothing more. For a time a federal law permitted unions to be incorporated in the District of Columbia, but this law was repealed in 1932.

Although a union may be the exclusive representative of all of the workers in a unit and therefore have the sole right to bargain for all the employees, it may refuse to admit to membership a significant group of the employees (for example, women) for whom it alone bargains. A union that refuses to admit Negroes nevertheless may be designated as the representative of all of the workers including Negroes. The NLRB will designate as the exclusive representative of a bargaining unit a union that refuses to admit Negroes and that even has requested that Negroes should not be included in the unit because it does not care to represent them. Under the Railway Labor Act the same thing can happen. A railroad labor organization can be designated as the exclusive bargaining representative of all the employees even though it will not admit Negroes. It is assumed that it will represent fairly those it will not admit to membership. How can anyone reasonably expect a union to represent without discrimination a group of employees that it does not even believe to be worthy of membership?

Generally speaking, the expulsion of employees from union membership has not been a direct concern of the federal government. The loss of membership to an employee is of especial importance where any form of closed-shop or maintenance-of-membership contract exists, because under such an agreement expulsion means the loss of employment to the worker involved. Most of the state courts show little interest in considering the rights of expelled members beyond ensuring that the procedures provided in the constitution of the union and by-laws are followed. The grounds for expulsion provided in the by-laws and constitution are generally of no concern to the state courts or to federal agencies. In some unions any criticism of a union official or the institution of a law suit against the union are grounds for expulsion. This hardly leads to responsible union organization and leadership.

Further, there are cases where labor unions are not actually responsible democratic organizations designed to reflect the wishes of their members. Infrequent conventions for the selection of officers in some cases are the rule. There are unions that greatly restrict the voting rights of some of their members, although the bargaining for such employees is done by agents who are not responsible to these groups of workers. Where these practices exist the objective of bargaining through unions of the employees' own choosing is far from a reality.

Neither the kinds of concerted action that a union has used nor the objectives that it has sought to attain by such weapons are now considered by the government in designating a given organization as the representative of a group of employees. The fact that a union calls a strike in violation of a federal law, that it uses concerted action to coerce an employer to violate a law, that it engages in work stoppages in violation of its agreements, and that it uses its economic power to restrict production and to impose inefficient processes on management have not been of any concern to the government in certifying it as a bargaining representative.

If the federal government is to protect the workers' right to organize and to engage in concerted action with its attendant consequences, and if the government confers the exclusive bargaining right on a majority union, it is only logical that it insist that a union receiving such rights should meet certain conditions that will further the national interest. The least it can do is to deny bargaining rights to any union that sets up arbitrary rules of admission that bar some of the employees in the unit that it desires to represent exclusively. Any union desiring to represent all employees must be willing to admit all employees. A labor organization that has the exclusive right to represent all employees cannot be considered to be merely a private social club. The government ought also to deny bargaining rights to unions that arbitrarily expel members for reasons unrelated to the performance of its bargaining role.

If one objective of the government's labor policy is to promote collective agreements, it would seem inconsistent and incongruous for the government to designate a union (or to permit it to continue to serve) as the exclusive representative of the workers in a bargaining unit if the courts have found that it has broken its collective agreements. The primary reason an employer is willing, apart from economic pressure, to sign a collective agreement with a union is because he believes that the contract will stabilize industrial relations in his establishment for its duration. If the bargaining union does not consider that the agreement is really binding, and if it is not willing to accept the obligations that the contract imposes upon it, that labor organization by its own action is running contrary to our national labor policy. To discourage such activities, a union that violates its agreements ought to be deprived of its bargaining rights for a given period of time.

It is inconsistent with our objective of minimizing industrial strife, for the government to confer exclusive bargaining rights on a union that engages in boycotts and sympathetic strikes. Such practices extend the area of a dispute to include parties who are not in any way directly related to the controversy and who can do nothing to settle the original dispute. Likewise, it is not in the public interest to permit a union to represent exclusively the employees in a unit if it attempts to impose upon the employer monopolistic practices that limit production or that increase the amount of human effort required per unit of output. Since it is generally agreed that an ever-increasing level of production is necessary for the attainment of a higher standard of living, and since it is desirable to reduce the human effort required in the productive process, such restrictive practices are opposed to the public interest.

The National Labor Relations Board should have the authority to refuse to certify (or to withdraw certification) as a bargaining representative any union that has adopted discriminatory conditions of admission or that expels members by arbitrary processes and on grounds not related to the performance of the bargaining function. Labor organizations that are set up in an undemocratic manner should also be denied bargaining rights.

The NLRB should have the authority to suspend bargaining rights of a union for a bargaining unit if it breaks contracts, employs coercive measures to secure the adoption of uneconomic methods of production, or engages in boycotts or violent picketing that affects the specific unit concerned.

If the members of a union break a contract, carry on a boycott, engage in sympathetic strikes, or picket in an undesirable manner, the union, to protect itself, ought to have an opportunity to expel the members who engage in such undesirable practices. Thus, it would be able to divest itself of the responsibility for the actions of such members. It would be unfair to hold a union responsible for the irresponsible conduct of its members if the labor organization did not authorize the acts and was willing to take steps to ensure that such persons should not continue to remain members of the organization.

Some may argue that the suspension of bargaining rights of a union under such circumstances would be a denial to workers of the right of self-organization. But the right of self-organization is not absolute. Where it stands in the way of the attainment of other objectives, it may have to give way. The suspension of bargaining rights of an organization does not mean that the employees it represents will lose their right to bargain collectively. They can always choose another labor organization to represent them.

CHAPTER XI

THE ORGANIZATION OF THE NATIONAL LABOR RELATIONS BOARD

The major task of positively enforcing the rights granted to labor to act concertedly has been conferred on the National Labor Relations Board. This Board now consists of three members appointed by the President with the consent of the Senate for five-year terms. The Board has the power to determine when violations of the National Labor Relations Act have occurred, to issue cease and desist orders to prevent future violations, and to direct employers to take remedial action to ensure that employees will be compensated for loss of wages resulting from employer interference with their right to engage in concerted action. These orders of the Board are enforced by a proceeding in the Circuit Court of Appeals. If the court believes the orders of the Board are in conformity with the law, it can secure compliance with them through the exercise of its contempt power. Is it desirable to continue the present machinery for enforcement of the law, or would modifications be advantageous?

DEFECTS IN THE PRESENT MACHINERY

A number of criticisms have been directed against the present method of enforcement. The operation of the National Labor Relations Board has been a source of much dissatisfaction. The present Board has repeatedly indicated that it considered its function to be to encourage the spread of unions. Certainly this attitude, as already indicated, is substantiated by certain provisions of the law and by some of the language in the reports of the congressional committees that considered this legislation. An examination of the congressional debates on the bill leads to the same conclusion. Many decisions of the Board appear to be founded on the premise that its function is to actively promote and encourage union organization.

129

A large number of the presumptions that it has set up for deciding cases can be justified only on this basis.

Our industrial relations program should be designed to protect workers in their right to engage in concerted activities. At the same time it must protect the public, employers, and other groups of employees from the potentiality of excesses and disruptions resulting from the use of concerted action. This goal differs fundamentally from the objectives of the present Board. Even though Congress should change the emphasis of the law, so as to make it clear that the purpose of the legislation is not to promote unions, but merely to permit them to operate where their objectives and methods are in the public interest, it is doubtful whether the present Board could completely free itself from the vast volume of precedents it has developed in the interpretation of the present law. The existence of these precedents would certainly be a barrier to the implementation of the program that is outlined here.

The procedures established under the National Labor Relations Act to enforce the orders of the Board make it possible to have an employer imprisoned without a jury trial for nonpayment of debt. This is surprising since imprisonment for debt has generally been abolished in this country. The awards of the Board are enforced through the contempt power of a circuit court of appeals, and any person who is in contempt of the court can be imprisoned. The imposition of money damages without a jury trial under this act has been upheld by the Supreme Court.[1] In the case involving this point, the Court held that the Seventh Amendment to the Constitution was not applicable. This amendment provides for a jury trial in all actions at common law where the amount involved is in excess of $20. The Supreme Court has held that the rights established by the NLRA are public and not private. The Seventh Amendment covers only private rights. The public nature of the rights under the law is not affected by the method of en-

[1] *NLRB* v. *Jones and Laughlin Steel Corp.,* 301 U.S. 1 (1937).

forcement which includes the payment of reparations to injured persons. Such reparations are not considered as satisfaction for private damages. The Supreme Court views it as a form of punishment designed to secure the enforcement of the public rights provided for in the act.

The Board has been criticized frequently because it is not bound by the rules of evidence normally applicable in the ordinary courts. The National Labor Relations Act clearly provides that the Board shall not be bound by the ordinary rules of evidence used in courts of law. As a consequence, not infrequently hearsay evidence is admitted to establish that a violation of the law has occurred. Many people believe that such hearsay evidence is not desirable, because the hearing officer does not have a chance to view the witness and thereby make his own judgment concerning the speaker's veracity, and also because the respondent is not in a position to cross-examine the original source of the evidence.

The amount of proof required to substantiate charges before the Board also has been a subject of complaint. The NLRA merely says that the decisions of the Board, if supported by evidence, should be enforced by the courts. What is meant by the phrase "if supported by evidence"—some evidence, substantial evidence, or a preponderance of evidence? At one time the Supreme Court held that decisions of the Board must be founded upon substantial evidence contained in its record. But more recently the Court has consistently held that if the Board had any evidence in the record to support its conclusions, the courts would not reverse the decision. This meant if the Court could find any evidence in the hearing that would tend to support the conclusions of the Board, the courts would uphold the decision, even though a preponderance of evidence in the record would not sustain the findings. As a result of the Administrative Procedure Act of 1946, the courts probably will change their attitude toward the amount of evidence required to support a finding of the Board. Section 7 (c) of this act provides that the determinations of all administrative bodies must be supported by "substantial evidence." This act would appear to apply to proceedings before the NLRB.

The charge has been made that the NLRB combines in itself the roles both of prosecutor and of judge. This criticism is well founded. All complaints are prosecuted in the name of the Board and by its attorneys. There is now a complete division between the sections of its staff that prosecute cases and those that take evidence in the proceedings. Nevertheless in the last resort the members of the Board are solely responsible for determining what complaints are to be prosecuted before it, as well as for the adjudication of those disputes. It would be only natural for a board to have some presumption in favor of a complaint that it had already decided was sufficiently well founded to be prosecuted.

Repeatedly it has been charged that the members of the National Labor Relations Board are prolabor. If its function is to promote labor organizations, it would have to be prolabor if it were to carry out the task imposed on it by Congress. Numerous members of the Board have from time to time spoken out in favor of promoting unions, and members who have taken an independent stand relative to the demands of labor have not been reappointed when their terms of service expired. A special House committee investigating the Board in 1939–40 presented much evidence showing that it was biased. Although the membership of the Board has changed since then, it is doubtful whether it is any less energetic in its efforts to carry out one of the major objectives of the act, that is, the spread of labor organizations.

Consequently, in the light of these defects in the present method of enforcing the NLRA, it would appear to be desirable to reappraise the problem of sanctions for securing compliance with the law. In place of the present machinery a number of choices are available. One method would be to impose on the ordinary civil and criminal courts the whole task of enforcing the rights of labor to engage in concerted action as well as the task of protecting the public from any possible excesses. There are several advantages in this approach. It would bring an end to the idea that the deciding agency should be the protagonist of one of the contending interests involved in the controversy. It would ensure the use of the ordinary rules of evidence that are applicable in court proceedings. All civil determinations would be based on factual conclusions supported by a preponderance of evidence, and in criminal cases it would require the proof of facts beyond a reasonable doubt. The respondent could demand a jury trial in both civil and criminal proceedings. Prosecuting and adjudicating functions would be completely separated.

Obviously this solution would involve some difficulties. The judicial process in the federal courts has frequently been slow. Industrial relations is a relatively specialized field, and many judges have little knowledge of the unique problems involved. If the task of enforcing these rights and obligations were imposed upon the federal judiciary, the views of prospective judges on labor relations might be a determining factor in their selection, because of the political power of organized labor. The tremendous political pressure that labor wields does not need to be demonstrated here. It would not be desirable to take any step that would encourage the selection of judges on the basis of their labor views rather than their over-all judicial competence.

Another method of enforcing these obligations would be to create a labor court. Such a court would have a specialized jurisdiction to enforce the duties imposed on both management and labor. Practically, this would mean converting the National Labor Relations Board into a court of specialized jurisdiction. In the fields of taxation, customs, patents, and claims against the government, such so-called legislative courts are now in existence. Although these bodies are actually courts, they can perform nonjudicial functions, which the constitutional courts are incapable of performing because of limitations imposed upon them by the Constitution. Obviously, the ordinary rules of evidence would be applicable in cases tried before such a tribunal; its findings in a civil case would have to be supported by a preponderance of evidence. Its decisions would be given judicial finality; and thus there would be no problem of appeal to other courts except in unusual instances. The establishment of a labor court implies a complete break with the basic philosophy underlying the National Labor Relations Act and the adoption of an entirely different approach to the problem than is proposed in this study.

Another method of enforcement would be to create a new administrative board whose decisions could be enforced in the district courts by an action to recover damages or by an order for compliance. This is similar to the method of enforcing the determinations of the National Railroad Adjustment Board and also the reparations orders of the Interstate Commerce Commission. The determinations of such a board thus would have only a *prima facie* validity, and in the enforcement proceedings, evidence could be introduced tending to disprove them. This would ensure that the final determination would be based at least on a preponderance of evidence and that it would be founded on facts established in accordance with the normal rules of evidence. But it would be a very cumbersome and costly procedure involving literally two trials. Obviously it would also be time-consuming.

RECOMMENDATION

The best method of meeting the problem would, we believe, be to abolish the present Board machinery and to create a new set-up along improved lines. It would be advantageous to enlarge the membership of the Board to seven or nine; at the same time it would be desirable to have cases heard by a single member, who would report to the full Board which would decide the case. This might mean a more speedy consideration of cases, and it would make possible, at least in many instances, the hearing of evidence by a Board member himself rather than by a trial examiner. It would be desirable for Congress to declare that all findings of fact of the Board or any member thereof must be based upon a preponderance of evidence, and to require that the Board follow the ordinary rules of evidence applicable in judicial proceedings. To prevent the merger of prosecuting and judicial functions in the same agency, the prosecution of cases before the Board should be put in a separate unit in the Department of Justice.

The new board of course should have the authority to impose reparation orders on whoever causes damages by violating the law. This should apply to labor as well as management. If unions engage in concerted action in violation of the law, they should pay damages to the employer, just as employers now have to recompense employees who suffer a loss because an employer interfered with their right to engage in concerted action.

It is believed that by taking these steps it would be possible to eliminate the shortcomings of the present Board, while still retaining the advantages of an administrative agency for the performance of this function. Thus the benefits of speed and expert knowledge that have come from the use of our administrative agencies could be attained without the shortcomings of the present Board.

CHAPTER XII

THE SETTLEMENT OF DISPUTES

The enormous economic and social losses that have resulted from industrial warfare in modern times have given rise to many efforts to remove some of the issues involved in disputes and to facilitate their peaceful settlement. The consequences of work stoppages in key industries are so grievous that many people have reached the conclusion that such cessations of work, must, by some means or other, be prevented.

Before considering the ultimate question of the permissibility of strikes, it is necessary to summarize briefly the nature of the existing government machinery for the removal of the causes of strikes and to facilitate the adjustment of controversies. We shall survey briefly the machinery under the National Labor Relations Act, the Conciliation Service, the Railway Labor Act, and the National War Labor Board. Attention will also be given to the adjustment of disputes in the White House, and the use of compulsory cooling-off periods. Desirable methods of settling disputes will be examined in the next chapter.

THE NATIONAL LABOR RELATIONS ACT

The National Labor Relations Act was designed to make it unnecessary for workers to engage in concerted activity in order to secure the enforcement of their right to join unions and to bargain collectively. When Congress made it illegal for employers to interfere with unions and to discriminate against workers because they joined unions, supporters of the legislation contended that it would automatically reduce strikes, because the workers' right to organize was now otherwise guaranteed. Even though administrative machinery was thus created to enforce the right to organize, Congress imposed no penalties on workers who still used concerted action.

136

Despite the creation of peaceful remedies for the enforcement of the right to organize, the man-days lost in strikes called between 1935–45 to enforce this right constituted a larger proportion of the man-days lost in strikes than was the case before. In the period from 1927–34 the number of man-days lost in organizational strikes was only 30 per cent of all the time lost in strikes, whereas in the period from 1935–45 it had increased to 54 per cent. This apparent anomaly resulted from the fact that the National Labor Relations Act placed primary emphasis on the spread of unionism. Workers were encouraged to continue to resort to the strike to speed up the organizational process. They were not deterred in using this method since no penalties were attached.

Meanwhile the number of man-days lost in strikes for all purposes greatly increased. The average number lost annually from 1927–34 in strikes called for all purposes was 12.5 millions, whereas in the period from 1935–45 the number had increased to 16.1 millions. Although one of the objectives of the act was to reduce strikes, the law nevertheless removed most of the risks from striking, and coupled with this it specifically provided that nothing in it limited the right to strike. The expansion in the number of union members made imperative the creation of adequate machinery for the peaceful settlement of disputes. The National Labor Relations Act did not provide machinery to facilitate such peaceful adjustment of controversies. Employers and employees had to resort to the machinery existing in the Conciliation Service for the voluntary adjustment of disputes.

THE CONCILIATION SERVICE

The United States Conciliation Service in the Department of Labor is probably the best example of a federal agency designed to facilitate the voluntary adjustment of disputes. The organic act of the Department of Labor (enacted in 1913) provides that one of the objectives of the Department is to conciliate labor disputes. Its activities in this field have steadily expanded so that there is hardly a major strike (outside the field of rail transportation) in which the Service does not attempt to facilitate a peaceful settlement. Neither the employers nor the employees are under any obligation to accept its good offices when it offers them, but rarely does anyone refuse to take advantage of the proffered services. The fear that the Conciliation Service will give adverse publicity to persons who refuse to accept its intervention tends of course to make both employers and employees accept its services.

Despite its record of expanding activities, the operation of the Conciliation Service appears to be seriously defective. Its location in the Department of Labor is a major source of difficulty. By law the Department is charged with the task of actively promoting the interests of workers. Secretaries of labor have on occasion said that in conciliating disputes it is the task of the Department to represent the interests of labor.[1] An agency attempting to conciliate disputes obviously has its efficacy reduced if it is obligated by law to promote the interest of one of the parties as against the other.

The second defect in its operations is its policy of pursuing peace at any price. Since the function of the Conciliation Service is to facilitate the peaceful settlement of disputes, it places primary emphasis upon the avoidance of or the rapid termination of a work stoppage, irrespective of the merits of the case. The attitude seems to be that any solution not illegal is desirable. This policy gives a great advantage to the party which makes the threat of breaking the industrial peace because that is the party which must be appeased. Since lockouts by employers were made illegal by the National Labor Relations Act, in practice the threat of a work stoppage always comes from labor. Under these circumstances, when the government attempts to facilitate a peaceful settlement by conciliation, it is in effect saying to the workers, "yes, of course

[1] *Third Annual Report of the Secretary of Labor* (1915), pp. 7–8.

you have the right to strike, but what does the employer have to give you to get you to refrain from exercising that right?"

The existence of these shortcomings in the Conciliation Service as it is now functioning does not indicate that attempts to conciliate labor disputes by the government have no place in the industrial relations program. Under certain conditions it is obviously to the advantage of the public to bring the parties to a dispute together so that they can at least negotiate and strive to arrive at a settlement.

RAILWAY LABOR DISPUTES

The Railway Labor Act of 1926 as amended contains a detailed program for the settlement of labor disputes on railroads and air lines. This machinery consists of the National Mediation Board, emergency boards, and the National Railroad Adjustment Board. In order to make possible the mediation of disputes before strikes develop, the law requires that all carriers and their employees must give to each other at least thirty days' notice of intended changes in working conditions. If a carrier fails to give such notice, criminal penalties are imposed, but no comparable penalties are provided for unions.

Should a dispute not be settled by direct negotiation between the parties, the National Mediation Board has jurisdiction to attempt to mediate it. The Board can assume jurisdiction on its own motion wherever it believes that a dispute might result in an interruption of interstate commerce. After the National Mediation Board takes a case under consideration, and for thirty days after it has completed action on it, neither party can change the conditions of employment except by mutual agreement. Thus the Board is in a position to attempt to mediate disputes before strikes have developed. If it fails in its efforts to mediate the dispute, it can offer arbitration. But a dispute can be submitted to arbitration only upon the agreement of both parties. If arbitration is not accepted, the jurisdiction of the Board is exhausted.

Should the Board fail in its efforts to attain a peaceful settlement, and should it find that an emergency exists, the President may appoint a special emergency board to report to him on the facts of the controversy and to make suggestions for a settlement. After the dispute has been referred to an emergency board, the conditions of employment cannot be changed for thirty days and must remain unchanged for another thirty days after the Board has rendered its report. But the law contains no provision for the enforcement of this section. There is nothing in the act that in any way limits the right of employees to strike. The recommendations of an emergency board constitute only advice; they are not binding on either party. It is assumed that public opinion will compel their acceptance.

The purpose of this act is to delay any change in the terms of employment until all possibilities for a peaceful settlement have been exhausted. By preventing the parties from changing the terms of employment by unilateral action, the law seeks to avoid the possibility that mediation might be interrupted by a strike while there is still a possibility of a peaceful settlement. If a strike is threatened after mediation has been exhausted, the theory is that an emergency board can make suggestions for a settlement that public opinion will force the parties to accept.

The National Mediation Board has been successful in mediating a large proportion of the cases that have come before it. Many of these have been minor disputes. The arbitration procedure provided by the Railway Labor Act has not been widely used. In only a small number of cases where the Board has suggested arbitration have both parties been willing to accept the proposal. In most instances the carrier, not the union, has been unwilling to arbitrate.

Until recently emergency boards, as a rule, have been able to prevent strikes on interstate carriers. Only about sixty emergency boards have been appointed under this act. Such a board, when appointed by the President, is directed first to attempt to mediate the dispute, and if this fails, it is instructed to investigate and report to the President on the issues involved. It can only present recommendations for the settlement of the dispute. Nothing in the law makes the recommendations of an emergency board binding on either party. In recent years neither labor nor the government has felt bound by the recommendations of emergency boards. In the general railway wage dispute of 1941, the unions were not satisfied with the recommendations of an emergency board and threatened to strike after the Board made its report. As a result of this threat the President intervened, the emergency board was directed to reconsider the matter, and it secured a settlement of the dispute on terms more favorable to the unions than were suggested in its original report.

Two years later when the nonoperating employees of all the major roads sought another wage increase, the government considered the recommendations of the emergency board to be undesirable, and the President acting under his war powers appointed a second board to reconsider the case. The workers refused to accept the recommendation of this new board. At about the same time another emergency board made recommendations concerning a dispute involving a request of the operating employees for a wage increase, and here again the workers were unwilling to accept its recommendations. Subsequently, both the operating and nonoperating workers, by threatening to strike, secured the intervention of the President, and through him they received more favorable terms of employment than were recommended by the boards. A similar situation developed in 1946, and by striking the workers were able to secure conditions of employment slightly better than an emergency board recommended. Several other strikes occurred on railroads and air lines, either before or after the appointment of an emergency board.

The National Railroad Adjustment Board constitutes the

third element in the machinery for the peaceful adjustment of railroad disputes. This Board is the only permanent agency in the United States that arbitrates cases, although one party does not desire it to do so. Its members are appointed by the carriers and unions, and when a deadlock develops between the representatives of the parties, an impartial chairman is designated to sit with the panel and settle the case. It has jurisdiction over all controversies between the carriers and their employees arising out of the interpretation and application of collective agreements. The jurisdiction of this Board is not exclusive. The employees can always strike in order to attempt to enforce their own interpretation of an agreement, and either side can sue in the courts instead of bringing a case before the Board. The decisions of the Board are enforced only by a proceeding in the appropriate United States District Court. Such an action for enforcement is the sole method of securing a judicial review of a decision of this Board.

Only when the employer refuses to carry out the terms of an award and the union actually seeks to enforce it judicially, can the employer secure a judicial review of the award of the Board. Otherwise the employer is unable to secure judicial review of an award. But in most cases where the carrier fails to comply with a decision, often because it is desirous of securing a judicial review, the union rarely uses the method of enforcement provided in the law. Generally, in such cases the labor organization threatens to strike and thereby ultimately secures the appointment of an emergency board to consider the matter in dispute. Not infrequently the emergency board recommends a settlement that is more advantageous to the workers. It should be remembered that the National Railroad Adjustment Board has jurisdiction only over disputes concerning rights under existing agreements. There is no machinery for the compulsory arbitration of disputes concerning interests.

These procedures contained in the Railway Labor Act were developed at the joint request of the carriers and the unions.

In rail transportation there has been a long tradition of collective bargaining, and the workers know that public opinion is opposed to work stoppages on any significant interstate carrier. The unions also are anxious to avoid strikes because their members fear a loss of seniority as a result of a strike, and under present operating rules, seniority is tremendously important.

Nevertheless, the workers are in a position to win a large part of their demands without making good a strike threat. Under our present system of industry-wide bargaining on rail carriers, a major strike would tie up almost all lines, and this would shortly bring the whole economy to a standstill. The National Mediation Board has been quite successful in settling most minor disputes by peaceful means. The major industry-wide controversies have generally gone to emergency boards before an acceptable solution was developed. Until recently the National Mediation Board and the emergency boards have generally been able to avert strikes. Labor peace on the rail carriers has probably been attained at some cost to the public, both as a consequence of increased wages and uneconomic working conditions. We are unable to assess the full extent of that additional cost to the public.

THE NATIONAL WAR LABOR BOARD

Only during major wars have we had machinery for the compulsory arbitration of disputes concerning interests. This function was performed by the National War Labor Board during World War II. The agency was first established by executive order in January 1942; later it received statutory authorization by the War Labor Disputes Act of 1943. The Board, composed of public, labor, and employer members all appointed by the President, had complete authority to settle finally any labor dispute likely to cause substantial interference with the war effort, and it considered that any controversy that might result in a strike would have that result. It could take jurisdiction over disputes submitted by either party, and it could also intervene in any case whether or not the parties desired it to do so. In settling such controversies, it was empowered to prescribe all conditions of employment that were involved. Neither by executive order nor by statute did the Board receive any direct power to enforce its decisions. But the President had authority to seize a war plant where production was likely to be interrupted by a labor dispute. The President sought to enforce the decisions of the Board by taking over the plant involved. This was done regardless of which party refused to obey the orders of the Board.

Actually this Board represented a mixture of mediation, compulsory arbitration, and regulatory action. By virtue of the Wage Stabilization Act of October 2, 1942, the Board was given authority to approve all wage changes (other than for salaried workers), even though they were voluntarily agreed to by employers and employees. Its functions under this act clearly were of a regulatory nature.

In dispute cases where it performed an arbitral function, the Board first attempted to mediate the controversy. The performance of the mediation function in such circumstances involved a number of difficulties. The Board took jurisdiction in most cases only after the Conciliation Service had failed in its attempt at mediation. Of course the parties knew that if the Board failed to settle a dispute through mediation, it could resolve it through compulsory arbitration. Thus the likelihood that the Board might impose its own judgment on the parties through arbitration always conditioned the performance of its conciliation function. This potentiality would make the parties more willing to accept its suggestions offered in mediation than if the same solution had been proposed by the Conciliation Service of the Department of Labor.

Congress never set forth the principles that the National War Labor Board was to apply in the settlement of disputes. In the field of wage determination it developed no clear-cut policies that it consistently applied in comparable cases. The

Board slowed up the increasing of wages that might have occurred during the war. But when it was confronted with difficult cases or disputes involving strong unions threatening to strike, it generally found a way to increase wages, even though it thereby disregarded principles that it had established in previous decisions.

When the National War Labor Board decided a case, it issued an order directing the parties to make a contract embodying the terms of its award. No machinery was provided for the direct enforcement of such decisions. Technically, the courts considered that the only function of the Board was to give advice to the President. If its award was not complied with, the President generally seized the property of the employer. In many instances this was done where it was actually the employees who refused to obey the directive of the Board. Obviously, since Congress did not make it illegal to strike, it was almost impossible for the government to enforce the decisions of the Board against unions.

The President empowered the Board to sequestrate union funds temporarily, to withhold money collected in a checkoff, and to cancel union-preference clauses in contracts where unions failed to abide by its decisions. But the executive order granting this authority provided that these steps could be taken only if the government had already seized the property of the employer. As a result of the nonapplication of sanctions against unions, a strong and determined labor organization could often defy the Board and secure what it desired. In 1944 and 1945 strikes not infrequently were called to get the Board to consider cases out of their normal order. Only because public opinion strongly opposed strikes during the war, was the Board able to operate and settle disputes with a minimum of work stoppages. With the termination of hostilities, it became apparent that labor was not willing to be bound by the awards of the Board, and consequently for this and other reasons it was abolished at the end of 1945.

THE PRESIDENT AND LABOR DISPUTES

Frequently, in the past fifteen years, the President has intervened directly in the settlement of labor disputes. Such presidential action has been primarily of three types: (1) the Chief Executive has attempted to mediate disputes directly or through certain specially selected agents. These attempts at mediation have had some success. (2) He has threatened to direct adverse publicity against participants who were unwilling to settle disputes by peaceful means. Not always have such efforts been successful, especially where it was a labor organization that was unwilling to use the available machinery for peaceful settlement. (3) On a number of occasions the President has urged the arbitration of disputes or has himself acted as an arbitrator. His efforts at personal arbitration at times have shown a lack of knowledge of the details and issues involved.

In fact, the President can exercise a considerable personal role in endeavoring to settle labor disputes. Not infrequently he has intervened before all other available peaceful remedies have been exhausted. The President has relied more upon his personal prestige than upon any specific grant of constitutional or statutory authority. Any President, if he so desires, can through the personal expression of opinion or through his influence on officials or government agencies facilitate the settlement of disputes. His ability to get results is conditioned by the political power of the parties to the controversy and by his knowledge of the problems involved.

COMPULSORY COOLING-OFF PERIOD

During World War II the federal government used another device to reduce the number of work stoppages. The War Labor Disputes Act of June 23, 1943, attempts to reduce strikes in war industries. It requires that the employees in a war industry can strike only after they have given thirty days' notice of their intention to do so. On the expiration of that period, the National Labor Relations Board is supposed to conduct a poll of the workers to determine whether or not they desire to strike. After such a ballot has been taken, the workers can strike whether or not a majority favors it. The only sanction compelling the workers to give such notice is the provision that the employers can sue the union for any damages incurred as a consequence of a strike not called in accordance with this act.

The theory of the act appears to be that in but few cases would a majority of the workers desire to strike if they had an opportunity to express their own wishes. The framers of the act seemed to assume that the existence of a cooling-off period between the time notice was given and the strike would reduce the number of work stoppages. But under this statute, giving notice of intention to strike became only a part of the bargaining process. In 1945, there were 1,445 strike ballots conducted, and in 1,249 of these elections a majority voted in favor of striking. But strikes followed the voting in only 213 of these situations. This would indicate that giving notice became a perfunctory step in the bargaining process.

This provision of the War Labor Disputes Act had in fact little effect on the number of strikes. Ninety-five per cent of the strikes in 1945 were called without paying any attention to the cooling-off requirement.

SUMMARY

The federal government has engaged in two primary methods of minimizing work stoppages; it has attempted to prevent some disputes from developing into strikes by removing their cause, and it has established machinery to facilitate the peaceful settlement of disputes either before or after a work stoppage has developed. The guarantee of the workers' right to organize, as contained in the National Labor Relations Act, is an example of an attempt to prevent disputes by removing the cause. The remedial approach has consisted mainly

of conciliation or arbitration. The National Railroad Adjustment Board and the National War Labor Board carried on
arbitration. Agencies engaged in conciliation have included
the President, the Conciliation Service, the Maritime Labor
Board, and the National Mediation Board.

Generally, government officials engaged in conciliation have
taken the attitude that the maintenance of industrial peace is
their primary objective. They assume that any concession not
illegal is justified if the granting of it will settle the dispute.
It is tacitly implied that no concession that is not illegal can
be as detrimental to the public as a work stoppage. Such a
policy of course confers some advantage on the party that is
threatening a breach of the industrial peace. Since practically
any form of concerted action by employers is illegal, only the
workers can threaten to break the peace by an overt act. Consequently, the attitude that industrial peace should be maintained at almost any cost confers a definite advantage on labor
in a dispute that is being mediated by the government.

The arbitration of labor disputes by the government is in
some cases compulsory and in other instances voluntary. Arbitration under the Railway Labor Act is completely voluntary.
The consent of both employers and employees is required. But
a dispute within the jurisdiction of the National Railroad Adjustment Board can be submitted to that body by either party.
Then the jurisdiction of the Board is obligatory on the other
party.

Controversies that are arbitrated fall into two classes: disputes concerning interests and disputes involving rights. Arbitration of disputes concerning rights consists of the interpretation of the terms of an existing agreement that is applicable
to a specific situation in dispute. This is the type of case
handled by the National Railroad Adjustment Board. The
arbitration of disputes concerning interests involves the determination of the terms to be included in a new contract when
the parties cannot reach agreement themselves. This is a more

difficult task than that involved in the arbitration of disputes concerning rights. In deciding this latter type of dispute, the arbitrator has the contract of the parties as a standard on which to base his decision. But in resolving a case concerning interests, there is no pre-existing standard to guide the arbitrator in determining what terms should be included in the new agreement.

On several occasions government agencies have attempted to combine conciliation and arbitration. An organization engaged in both of these functions finds it difficult to perform either of them successfully. The aim of a conciliator should be to bring about a settlement of the dispute. In his opinion almost any terms are desirable if their acceptance will preserve or restore industrial peace. But the aim of the arbitrator should be a sound settlement of the dispute on the basis of its real merits. If in arbitrating a dispute the agent follows the techniques of the conciliator, he may be charged with inconsistency, but if in conciliating he attempts to adhere to the principles that he applied in arbitrating other disputes, he is open to the charge of being prejudiced in advance.

CHAPTER XIII

HOW CAN INDUSTRIAL DISPUTES BE SETTLED?

The fundamental national goal of steadily rising standards of living for the masses can be realized in full measure, only provided disruptions of production resulting from industrial warfare can be localized and minimized. In a complex, highly integrated, economic system, the rate of advancement will inevitably be retarded, so long as stoppages of work occur in key industries. Strikes in any important industry commonly mean serious interference with production in many related industries. In the case of a vital public service, the entire productive process may be disrupted.

Employers, workers, and the general public all have a stake in restricting industrial warfare and minimizing the disruption of production. The interests of the three groups are, in the long run, mutual. That is to say, without steadily expanding production, the public cannot obtain a greater volume of goods and services, nor can profits and wages be progressively increased. All groups benefit by the elimination or reduction of industrial warfare.

It remains true nevertheless that at any given moment the interests of the several groups do not coincide. The workers desire immediate advances in money wages, or shorter hours, or improved working conditions, with little regard for the interests of the employer and the public; the employer naturally desires to maintain or improve his profit position; while the public wishes to reap the benefit of lower prices. However, the public is ordinarily not a participant in the wage contract and has no voice in the decision reached.

Because the wage contract is made for a relatively short period, union officials naturally have a short-run view. Their prestige depends upon their success in obtaining with each new contract maximum wage increases. Consequently, year after year emphasis is placed upon the rapid increase in money wages, without much reference to the state of technological progress. In this struggle the strike is naturally looked upon as the primary weapon in the arsenal of labor. Similarly, employers have long regarded the lockout as a legitimate weapon.

The ultimate question with which we are faced in this analysis is, How can industrial disputes be adjusted so as to minimize the stoppages of production? There are just two methods by which industrial disputes may be adjusted: one is by negotiation and agreement between the contending parties; the other is by the imposition of terms by the government. The first method takes the form of collective bargaining; the second of compulsory arbitration either by means of special boards or by regularly constituted industrial courts. The problems involved in these alternatives will be briefly analyzed.

COMPULSORY SETTLEMENTS

Compulsory arbitration involves the determination by a government agency of all the terms of employment that are in dispute between an employer and his employees. The arbitral agency embodies its decision in an award that is absolutely binding on all the parties to the dispute. Employees cannot strike if they are dissatisfied, nor can employers resort to a lockout if they are not pleased with the award. The process of compulsory arbitration is beset with at least four difficulties:

(1) There are no generally accepted standards for settling industrial disputes. Only where such standards exist, can disputes be settled fairly and the participants be convinced of the fairness of the decision. If comparable cases are to be decided in a comparable manner, principles of decision must be established in advance. The principles now used by arbitrators to settle wage disputes clearly indicate the absence of any generally accepted applicable standards. Numerous principles for adjusting wages have, however, been employed.

Splitting the difference is one of the most common methods of settling such controversies. The arbitrator grants a wage increase approximately half way between what the employees demand and what the employer is willing to give. Obviously a decision made in this way takes no account of the specific merits of the case. This principle merely encourages both parties to take absurd bargaining positions.

The rate of pay prevailing for comparable work is commonly used by arbitrators as a basis for fixing wages. This standard can be used only when there is a free market in which going rates of pay have been established by voluntary bargaining. If arbitration becomes compulsory and general, there is no going wage rate in a free market that can be used as a standard.

Arbitrators frequently adjust wages on the basis of changes in the cost of living. Such a basis of decision takes no account of the employer's capacity to pay the wage. It assumes as desirable the standard of living existing in the base period used. A rigid application of this principle would preclude the workers from ever receiving as wages any of the gains resulting from technological progress.

In the industrial controversies of 1946, certain new conceptions appear. The first is that the true test of an appropriate wage is not the prevailing rate in the industry but what the individual company can afford to pay in the light of its profit situation. This was illustrated in the General Motors automobile case. A second principle was that entire industries should make uniform increases in pay irrespective of variations in conditions. In practice, this implied that the wage increase should be based on the ability to pay of the more prosperous concerns. Third, it was assumed that all of the technological gains of industry should accrue to labor—with employers and the consuming public obtaining none of the benefits.

If governmental decisions on such issues are to be other than arbitrary, it is obviously necessary that the board, the fact-finding committee, the President, or the court should be in a position to determine with some degree of accuracy the profit potential of the industry and the company over the period covered by the wage agreement. Any decision concerning ability to pay involves analysis and appraisal of complex fact situations with respect to costs, prices, and future demands. This task is impossible for either a specially appointed fact-finding board or a permanent board or court. It is difficult enough for the industrial managers whose entire time is devoted to this task. Even they find it necessary to revise their judgments in the light of constantly changing conditions with respect to market demands, competition, and changes in cost.

Decisions based upon capacity to pay—whether of the company or the industry—inevitably involve judgment as to what profits are proper. This is because in any given situation the decision as to what a company can afford to pay necessarily includes consideration of how much profit is essential for continued operation and expansion.

In discussing the problem of standards used in arbitration, it is necessary to distinguish between the arbitration of disputes involving rights and those involving interests. One of the best examples of arbitration of disputes concerning rights is the settlement of controversies regarding the interpretation and application of the terms of existing contracts. Here the provisions of the contract constitute a pre-existing standard to guide the arbitrator in reaching a decision. But in settling a dispute concerning interests, such as the terms of a future contract, there is no pre-existing standard applicable. The task performed by arbitrators in settling disputes regarding interests differs greatly from the task performed by an ordinary court of law. Courts of law apply pre-existing rules of law to specific fact situations. In this process there is very little room left for arbitrary discretion upon the part of the judge. But in arbitrating disputes concerning interests, the arbitrator is left with wide discretion. Because of the absence of pre-existing standards, it is practically impossible to treat comparable cases in a comparable way as is done in a court of law.

(2) Arbitration decisions would commonly be colored by considerations of political expediency. The absence of specific, concrete standards to guide arbitrators in deciding cases means that they could settle them in an arbitrary way. In an industry-wide dispute involving large numbers of workers, political considerations would often be important. Decisions that would be displeasing to large masses of workers would be deemed politically undesirable. The arbitrator would be interested in a peaceful settlement of a dispute, but he would also be interested in a settlement that would be acceptable to the large number of workers involved.

(3) Compulsory arbitration leads ultimately to general government control of industry. The board of arbitration would have to settle any kind of a dispute that arose between employers and employees. If the workers opposed the introduction of a given labor-saving device, the board of arbitration would have to determine whether this change would be desirable. If an employer desired to move his plant from one city to another regardless of the workers' interests, the arbitrator would have to decide whether the change in location would be appropriate. In determining whether a given wage increase would be proper, the board would have to determine whether the employer could afford to pay the increase demanded. The measure of his ability to pay would be conditioned by what the board of arbitration considered to be an appropriate profit. If technological gains were available for distribution, the board would have to decide how much of them should go to workers in the form of higher wages, how much to the owners in the form of higher profits, and how much to the consumers in the form of lower prices.

(4) A prohibition of strikes is not readily enforceable. Any program of compulsory arbitration would require the com-

plete prohibition of strikes. Arbitration awards must be binding on both employers and employees. Since such decisions would be applicable in the future, it would be necessary to prevent the parties from avoiding them by terminating the employment relationship. Employers would have to be prohibited from closing down to avoid compliance, and workers would have to be prohibited from quitting if they were dissatisfied.

As a practical matter, no one has as yet been able to devise a system of penalties that would effectively prohibit strikes in disputes concerning interests. The Commonwealth of Australia has had a system of compulsory arbitration and a complete prohibition of strikes for over forty years. In Australia the time lost in strikes is as great as in this country when allowance is made for the difference in population. Because of political considerations, the penalties designed to prohibit strikes seldom have been applied against the workers.

In the United States during World War II, many strikes occurred, although the National War Labor Board was acting as a board of arbitration, and strikes were supposedly regarded as highly undesirable if not completely illegal. As the war continued, the time lost in strikes progressively increased. No penalties were applied against unions which struck rather than resort to the National War Labor Board or which refused to accept the decisions of the Board. Strong and determined unions repeatedly secured more favorable terms by the use of the strike than would have been justified under the precedents of the National War Labor Board. It should also be remembered that the penalties against strikes in violation of the War Labor Disputes Act were seldom applied.

COLLECTIVE BARGAINING

The only alternative to government determination of the terms of employment is private agreements reached between the parties at interest, through the processes of collective bargaining. This is the method that has traditionally been employed in the United States and that has been deemed to be in accord with American conceptions and practices. The making of agreements through collective bargaining has certain definite advantages, and it also admittedly has certain shortcomings.

The primary advantage of the collective bargaining process is that the agreements reached generally reflect economic conditions and factors at the company and in the area where the dispute occurs. The theory of collective bargaining is that the negotiations between an employer and his employees take account of such factors as the current financial position of the company and its requirements for expansion programs; the immediate business situation and outlook; the relative position of the workers as compared with others in the industry and in the area; and the degree of efficiency. The general condition of business and the labor market situation are often factors of decisive importance. In periods of good business and labor scarcity, the bargaining position of labor is usually relatively strong; when business is dull or receding and the supply of labor is abundant, the position of the employer is relatively strong.

If the collective bargaining agreements are to be sound, that is, in accordance with economic realities, the bargaining obviously must be between groups of comparable strength. Under the individual bargaining process the position of the workers was of course very weak, except in boom times when alternative employment was abundant. Under collective bargaining the position of labor has been greatly strengthened, but until recent times it still remained weaker than that of the employer. The labor negotiators were inexperienced, and they had meager financial capacity with which to meet the sacrifices involved in work stoppages. With the evolution of nationwide unions, however, the position of labor was greatly strengthened in both respects. Indeed, as we have seen, national labor organizations now commonly hold the whip-hand in dealing with individual employers, especially when they are backed by the power of government.

Since labor agreements cannot work satisfactorily unless they are based upon economic realities, they should obviously be made between the employers and the employees of a given company. The company not the industry is the unit of production; and it is in the individual company that wages are paid and profits are made—or losses incurred. Moreover, it is only in the individual company that mutual understanding and co-operation between management and labor can be worked out. It is there that the practical problems confronting both labor and management arise, and hence it is only there that realistic solutions can be obtained.

We are not suggesting that national labor organizations should be broken up nor that nation-wide employers associations should be dissolved. All groups in the body politic have the right to form organizations of whatever scope the members desire. We are merely insisting that the wage contract should be made between each company and its employees—for it is the productive operations of the individual company which creates both wages and profits. (For further discussion of this subject, see pages 61–65.)

Collective bargaining on the company basis is also indispensable for the protection of the public. When the bargaining process involves all of the companies in an industry, the stoppage of work will profoundly affect the welfare of the general public. When it is confined to a given company, the public may be inconvenienced, but as a rule only a small part of the industry is closed down at one time. Under this method it would be only in exceptional cases, involving chiefly local utilities, that the welfare of the public would be seriously imperiled.

It should be clearly recognized that collective bargaining, in contrast with compulsory arbitration, implies the use of the strike and the lockout as legitimate weapons. It should be recognized that employees have the right to strike to enforce their demands and that employers have a comparable right to close their plants. Obviously, it is not to the advantage of either party to use these methods except as a last resort.

PROTECTION OF THE PUBLIC

Adherence to the collective bargaining principle does not necessarily mean that the number and the scope of work stoppages cannot be reduced and the public thereby protected. Public opinion apparently will support limitations on the use of the strike in certain circumstances. Strikes that are not a necessary part of the bargaining process, that are designed to injure third parties, and that are used where an adequate peaceful remedy for settling the matter exists should be declared contrary to public policy. As was suggested in Chapter VII, the right to engage in concerted action could legally be restricted in a dispute where an adequate peaceful remedy for settlement exists. Thus strikes for organizational purposes could be penalized because the National Labor Relations Act provides a peaceful remedy. Strikes to enforce a given interpretation of an existing contract ought to be punished, because courts are available for the interpretation and application of agreements. Where the objective of a strike is illegal, as, for example, to secure a closed shop, the work stoppage could be penalized. The use of force and violence in a dispute ought to be made illegal. Sympathetic strikes and jurisdictional strikes could be outlawed without impairing the bargaining power of workers, because there is nothing that the employers involved in such disputes can do to settle them. Likewise, secondary boycotts could be prohibited, for the immediate objective of such activities is the injury of innocent persons not connected with the original dispute.

To penalize these undesirable activities a number of steps could be taken: (1) employers should be permitted to discharge employees who engage in such practices; (2) the bargaining rights of the union concerned should be suspended or abrogated; and (3) the employer should be permitted to recover from the union any damages that he suffered thereby. In short, the use of work stoppages should be permitted only in cases involving direct conflict over the terms of employment.

The public can also be protected by limiting the power of labor organizations to tie up the entire production in an industry at one time. When concerted action is directed against all producers in an industry, a work stoppage can profoundly affect the welfare of the general public. To reduce the possibility of an entire industry being tied up at one time, this study has suggested that two steps be taken. First, as recommended in Chapter VII, unions should be made subject to the antitrust laws. This would restrict their monopoly powers. As a part of this process, the law should specifically declare that it is illegal for labor organizations to carry on concurrent concerted actions against two or more employers in the same industry, at the same time, as part of a general program. This would make unlawful a centrally planned program designed to shut down many producers at the same time. Second, as suggested in Chapter IX, the National Labor Relations Board should be prohibited from designating bargaining units that include employees of more than one employer. If these steps are taken, the possibility of industry-wide stoppages will be reduced.

For collective bargaining to operate effectively in settling disputes, both employers and employees must be required to bargain collectively. At present only employers are required to do so. Labor organizations are not obligated to bargain. They can strike without even stating their demands. As was recommended in Chapter VIII, it is necessary to impose the obligation to bargain on both the employer and the union.

As a part of a program for settling disputes by collective bargaining, it would be desirable to create improved governmental machinery to assist in the voluntary adjustment of disputes. It would be advantageous to ensure that the parties involved in a controversy were actually attempting to solve it. Although the existing Conciliation Service has performed useful functions, it needs reorganization. Its operation has suffered from two primary defects: first, it is a part of the Department of Labor, which is expressly charged with the primary task of promoting the interests of the workers; a second shortcoming is its underlying philosophy of peace at any price.

The performance of the conciliation function by the national government could be greatly improved by a few changes. The Conciliation Service should be removed from the Department of Labor. Its functions should be performed by an independent agency, headed by a board of three or five members, all of whom should be completely disassociated from employer and employee interests. Congress should clearly state that it is not the function of this agency to promote the interest of either party. The legislature must indicate that peace at any price should not be its policy.

If the parties to a dispute voluntarily agree to submit it to arbitration, the federal government should facilitate the process. Agreements to arbitrate normally are not considered to be enforceable contracts. The United States Arbitration Act of 1925 does not specifically cover arbitration provisions of labor contracts. The exemption of such agreements in this field was included in this act at the insistence of organized labor. As a result, except in the railroad field, collective agreements to arbitrate labor disputes are not regarded as enforceable contracts in the federal courts. It is desirable that agreements to arbitrate labor disputes be enforceable in the federal courts so far as they come within their jurisdiction.

If the suggestions here advanced to limit the use of strikes should be adopted, it is believed that the number and severity of work stoppages would be very greatly curtailed. However, it must be recognized that work stoppages might still occur.

Great public inconvenience and injury could result from a strike on an important railroad or against a significant utility company. Even though all of the suggestions here advanced were adopted, it might happen that the public would be deprived of a vital service over a long period. But it is believed such inconvenience is less undesirable in the long run than the consequences of the determination of the terms of employment by the government. Where great public injury is threatened by a stoppage, the law-making branches of the government— including both Congress and the President—would be expected to step in to meet the specific emergency involved. But it would be highly undesirable to adopt any program that would encourage either party to a dispute to seek government intervention to settle it.

INDEX

American Federation of Labor, 2, 3, 7, 8, 13, 17, 29, 33, 42, 110
American plan, 6
Anti-Racketeering Act, 44
Arbitration, 140, 148, 160
  compulsory, 144–45, 151–55, 157

Bargaining power, 20, 26, 28, 29, 49, 89–90, 113, 116, 117–18
Bargaining units, 9, 25, 28, 43, 110–23
Boycotts, 22, 23, 65, 94–96, 127–28

Checkoff, 82–84
Closed shop, 4, 9, 22, 23, 24, 29, 36, 42, 79–80, 100
Collective agreements, 24, 90, 156
  enforcement of, 25, 27, 107–08
  scope of, 105–06
  violation of, 91, 126
  written, 101
Collective bargaining, 9, 24, 34, 61–64, 98–109, 155–60
Company unions, 7
Compulsory settlement, 151–55
Conciliation, 66, 159
Conciliation Service, 27, 28, 137–39, 148
Congress of Industrial Organizations, 7, 17, 29, 33, 42
Constitution, 20, 21, 23
Cooling-off period, 146
Cost of living, 152

Discipline of employees, 75
Disputes,
  concerning interests, 153
  concerning rights, 153
  settlement of, 26, 65, 136–60

Eastman, Joseph B., 47
Emergency boards, 140–41
Employee representation plans, 7
Employees,
  discharge of, 93–94, 158
  expulsion from unions of, 125–26
  minority groups of, 112
  on strike, 88–89
  reinstatement of, 89

union discrimination against, 125, 128
Employers, 99–100
  interference with right to organize, 77–78
  obligation to bargain, 99–100
  prerogatives of, 105–06
Evidence, rules of, 131

Fact-finding committees, 41
Foremen, 105
Freedom of organization, 20, 113, 121–23
Freedom of speech, 53, 72–73, 92

Gompers, Samuel, 2
Good faith in collective bargaining, 100
Green, William, 2

Hillman, Sidney, 17

Industry-wide bargaining, 33, 43, 61–64, 65, 91, 117–20, 121, 122, 157
Injunctions, 87

Labor, Department of, 35, 43, 138
Labor court, 133–34
Lea Act, 45
Lewis, John L., 31, 36, 37, 104
Little Steel Formula, 18, 38
Lockout, 27, 118

Maintenance of membership, 23, 80
Majority rule, 28, 111–12, 124
Monopolies, labor, 64, 81–82, 159
Murray, Philip, 46

National Defense Mediation Board, 17, 36
National income, 50, 56
  distribution of, 51, 57
National Industrial Recovery Act, 10, 12, 13
National Labor Relations Act, 14, 15, 24, 25, 70, 81, 83, 136–37
  amendments to, 44, 136–37

163

National Labor Relations Board, 15, 22, 28, 42, 99–102, 113–17
  defects of, 129–32
  enforcement of orders of, 130–31
  members of, 132
  reorganization of, 132–35
National Mediation Board, 8, 39, 119, 139
National Railroad Adjustment Board, 134, 141–42
National War Labor Board, 18, 19, 80, 119, 143–45
Negroes, 125
Norris-LaGuardia Anti-Injunction Act, 9, 10, 86, 95

Organize, right to, 22, 25, 28, 52, 69–79

Peaceful settlement of disputes, 20
Perkins, Frances, 35
Picketing, 22, 23, 45, 92–94
Political Action Committee, 32, 40, 45
Politics, 31, 42, 154
Politics, and industry-wide bargaining, 62–63
Preferential hiring, 79–80
President, 34, 37, 38, 41, 145–46
Production, 58–60
  efficiency of, 61–62
  restriction of, 59

Railway Labor Act, 8, 22, 25, 38, 69, 80, 83, 106–07, 139–43
Roosevelt, Franklin D., 35

Sherman Antitrust Act, 86, 90, 103, 118
Standards of living, 50
Strike,
  limitation of right to, 86–88
  right to, 26, 85–86

Strikes, 22, 23, 33, 45, 85–94, 154–55
  jurisdictional, 65, 75–76, 90, 95, 158
  number of, 137
  organizational, 76, 78–79, 158
  sit-down, 35
  sympathetic, 64, 90, 127, 158

Technological changes, 5, 52, 59, 121–22
Truman, Harry L., 39, 40

Union preference agreements, 23, 30, 79–84
Union shop, 79
Unions,
  admission to, 126–28
  and collective bargaining, 103–04
  bargaining rights of, 127
  craft, 3, 7, 115
  functions of, 55–58
  industrial, 115
  interference with organization of, 73
  members, discrimination against, 73–74
  membership, 4, 5, 17, 31
  nature of, 125
  restrictive practices of, 58–60
  suability of, 107–09
  unaffiliated, 29, 30

Violence, 53, 64, 87, 89

Wages, 52, 57, 58, 62, 63
  capacity to pay, 152–53
  guaranteed, 106
  prevailing, 152
Wallace, Henry A., 41
War Labor Disputes Act, 18, 87–88, 143, 146
World War I, 3, 4
World War II, 17, 36, 155

Yellow-dog contracts, 10